Dedications

This book is dedicated to my three boys, Brian, Kieth, and Scott, and all of my friends, peers, and employees who tolerated my passion for business and pursuit of success.

Ron Sturgeon

Preface

A Word From

Ron Sturgeon

The original idea to write this book came many years ago, when a friend in the floral industry asked me what he could do to grow his business. He recognized that, although I didn't have much in the way of a formal education, I had achieved unusual success as an entrepreneur. He believed that the principles I had applied to build a successful auto recycling business could be learned and applied by any business owner. I share that belief.

Over time, I have encountered many other small business owners in various industries with the same question my friend asked. They want to know how to improve their business; they dream big and want to grow their businesses in leaps and bounds, not fits and starts. These business people don't want theories; they want actionable advice and real-world techniques. They aren't afraid to get their hands dirty and do whatever it takes to get to where they want to be. They are the people I originally wrote this book for.

I've found that many owners of small businesses out there want more success than they currently have and are willing to do whatever is necessary to achieve it. The problem is, they don't know what to do next! In the six years since this book was first published, I've seen first-hand how eager the owners of small businesses are for practical business advice. This book has been reprinted three times and is licensed for publication in five languages. In addition, the reception this book received led me to write a second book, Green Weenies and Due Diligence, an insider's guide to business jargon that was published in 2005.

Under the banner of "Mr. Mission Possible," I have a busy schedule as a consultant, mentor, and public speaker. These venues allow me to expand upon and illustrate the principles that anyone can use to make their small businesses more successful and efficient. Since I first wrote this book, I have started new ventures that include a salvage auto auction, an exotic car rental company, timeshare & driving event product.

Because of my success, people often approach me and ask for the keys to such accomplishments. As you begin reading this book, I'd say that these are the four most important secrets to my success:

- Read Everything Business Related
  I am self-taught on virtually everything. The material is out there, but in order to learn it all, you must become a voracious reader.

- Exercise the Willingness to Work Hard
  I don't necessarily mean manual labor - although I certainly did plenty of that when I was young! Be willing to put in the time; even reading can be hard work.

- Develop Excellent Marketing Skills
  In today's world, you have to market your business and yourself. Take advantage of the Internet and the many new ways it offers to promote yourself and your business. If you're not tech savvy, hire someone to teach you.

- Don't Just Be a Boss - Become an Effective Leader
  Almost anybody can be a boss, but it takes someone exceptional to become a leader. Make it your goal not only to achieve success for yourself, but also to inspire others to do the same - and then lead by example.

As you read this book, keep these four keys in mind. They have been the foundation to my success. Applied with diligence, these keys and the other principles in this book can be the foundation for your success as well.

Forward

by

Paula Felps

The first time I met Ron Sturgeon, I was on an assignment for a luxury car magazine. Originally, I was supposed to write a story about Ron and his impressive assortment of high-end automobiles, but I soon discovered that the cars in his garages were just the tip of the iceberg. The story quickly took a new direction, and his unique collection of antique toy cars ended up taking center stage - with an almost casual mention of his collection of "real" cars.

That's pretty typical for Ron; with every encounter, you get a little bit more than you bargained for and you come away with something a little bit different than you expected. And the same can be said of this book - while you might pick it up for one specific reason, you're going to end up learning something else that you didn't expect.

Ron has become a mentor and teacher for individuals from all walks of life and from every imaginable profession. At social events hosted by Ron, I've been surprised (and always enlightened) by the disparate range of backgrounds, interests and professions of the people I've met. Because he isn't your average success story, Ron truly believes that anyone who wants to can succeed - and he is determined to help them do so. I've met and interviewed many successful people, but have never met anyone as passionate as Ron is about helping others succeed.

It doesn't matter what business you're in; Ron's tools for success are universal and can be applied to anyone who has the determination and dedication to pick them up and use them as directed. He isn't afraid to dream big, and he encourages everyone he meets to dream just a big as he does. Given all that he has accomplished, it's useless to argue that it won't work - Ron is living proof that it does. Big thoughts accomplish big results, and the success that Ron enjoys is larger that life.

One of Ron's greatest gifts is his ability to take large, complex business concepts and break them down into understandable tasks and attainable goals. He is able to explain complicated procedures in a way that makes them seem less intimidating and more accessible. This book is a brilliant example of that ability.

Regardless of what your goals are or what kind of business you run (or want to run), Ron's insight is applicable and easily appreciated. Ron loves questions: He loves asking them and he loves answering them. How To Salvage More Millions From Your Small Business is like sitting down with him and tapping into more than three decades of business experience. He'll provide you with questions you never thought of asking, and answers that he discovered through trial and error. But most of all, he'll make you understand why he's called "Mr. Mission Possible."

If you've got the dream and the desire to make your small business succeed, make sure this book is part of your toolbox. It might not be the only book you'll ever need, but it is certainly one that you don't want to miss.

Take Action to achieve significant success, using the action work sheet on page 215. this handy sheet will guide you; with references back to the page number that discusses needed actions. Just sit down, enter reasonable dates for beginning (its ok to cheat and allow a little too much time, you don't want to try to do too much all at once, and then become frustrated.) Remember significant success doesn't happen overnight, and it's within your control!

Table Of Contents

Salvaging More Millions From Your Small Business

Chapter 1

Chapter 2

Table Of Contents

Table Of Contents

Table Of Contents

Table Of Contents

Table Of Contents

Table Of Contents

Chapter I

It's About Money

This chapter is about understanding the importance of your financial statement. It is also a look at the importance of operating metrics and how to use them. If you never open a financial statement but just track the metrics, you can get useful results as long as the metrics you're tracking are the right ones and you make adjusted decisions as you go along.

Profit is the difference between all costs and net sales. You make profit by tracking and controlling numbers, and by watching the costs of daily operation and making decisions accordingly.

Most people don't understand financial statements. If you're one of those people, get the help you need to understand them. Find out how. There are many courses offered by local colleges and schools. There are also numerous books on the subject. Go to a professional accountant or CPA for knowledge in this area. The most important thing in your bid for profit is grasping the importance of this essential tool. Don't be intimidated by financial statements, and remember, the metrics can be fun.

We're not going to teach you how in this book, but we certainly want to impress upon you the importance of gaining this understanding.

In our experience, most small business owners don't produce monthly financial statements, and, if they do, the statements are usually dumped in the trash or filed away for tax season. They are not analyzed, as they should be. This is a mistake. Monthly statements, when understood, can produce a bevy of financial clues.

Remember, profit is the difference between all costs and net sales. If you are not monitoring expenses within your cash flow, you will not discern errors in your decision-making. You are likely going to miss the important reasons why you are making or not making a profit.

If you're not monitoring how profit is made, you're not monitoring how loss is created. How can you expect to manage your operation toward profit if you are not tracking revenues and monitoring expenditures? It's the only way you'll make decisions correctly.

There's a signpost at the top of your long

Tool

If you are unfamiliar with how to set up and use a financial statement, seek professional assistance and begin at once keeping this important management tool.

climb. It points the way toward significant success. You'll discover you've got to climb a few hills before you actually reach that treasured place.

To go uphill to the first sign, you'll have to monitor your uphill progress. Otherwise you'll either sidetrack or turn downward by degrees. A typical statement from a side-tracker is, "I don't understand how I can work so hard and still not make it." This person has ambition but has never bothered to develop a way of monitoring his or her uphill progress.

Most individuals are better off going to a professional because of the hands-on relationship in the teaching process that they can then apply to their specific situation. Not everyone is inclined to hire help however, even when they should. Many are reluctant to spend the $300 to $500 in monthly fees for an accountant or other professional while they learn because they don't understand how much money they're losing by not doing so. Many individuals will go to software or books, striving to teach themselves. For a few that can be effective, but you'll learn faster by going to a pro.

Action!

To encourage the proper use of financial statements, schedule your meetings with your accountant once a month.

For those who use an accountant, we suggest you go over your financial statement with him or her for at least 30 minutes every month until you understand the statements yourself. This person can show you things you could otherwise take quite a long while to discover on your own. The accountant can answer your questions as you go through the learning tree of understanding. It's to your advantage to use a professional guide early on. Once you believe you have a working knowledge of a financial statement, you can take it on yourself and create a habit of analyzing it.

Your monthly financial statements are a road map of your progress. They will show you when you are stuck or going backwards. Use them to your advantage.

If you decide to use software in-house, you're better off to find someone who knows how to use its real potential. Don't experiment by teaching yourself. This knowledge is too important to your business. Your profit and eventual success both depend in a large part on whether or not you gain this understanding.

Once you begin to gain this knowledge, we suggest you consider distributing at least some of that information in the financial statement to your managers and employees. If some degree of privacy is a concern, then distribute only those line items that are important to the management of your firm or the line items that are within the control of these employees.

The information provided by your financial statement will uncover the reasons why your operation is not making a profit, why it's digressing.

Tool

Give your managers financial figures that will help them realize and focus on goals that will propel you toward the profits of a successful business.

Action!

Resolve to study your financial statements and operating metrics monthly.

Want to go uphill? Learn to read and use your monthly financial statements.

Use Operating Metrics

The use of operating metrics may be even more important for attaining success than the regular monitoring of financial statements. Why? Operating metrics provide a measure of the performance of your management decisions as you go along.

If such metrics are available for your industry, get them! Your trade association can probably provide a set of important things to monitor based on the general terms of your industry. Ask your accountant for industry standards.

If you're not in the auto recycling industry, you can run a parallel to what we consider in our profits:

- # vehicles bought for salvage
- # vehicles dismantled per employee
- # invoices written per day
- # customer calls
- # sales per day
- # sales per salesperson

That's a picture of operating metrics. They are generally kept in a spreadsheet either on a computer or in a notebook.

Tool

The use of operating metrics is more intuitive than it is intimidating. Create your first metrics study today. Your goal is to learn to see your business in numbers. Limit your metrics to a small number of items, less than 10 to start. Add or delete categories as the numbers begin to make sense. You'll soon discover what's important to you.

It's not hard to figure out what's important to your business. Just think about those actions and expenses that can be affected by a decision. Ask yourself a question or two like this: What can I change that could add to my profits?

You can always benchmark off other businesses by comparing your operation to others. In fact, it's a healthy thing to ask some of your associates or business friends in other industries what they monitor in order to better understand their business.

Don't spend a lot of time tracking meaningless data. You can refine the information you're tracking as you go along. Try to keep the final number of items to less than a dozen. Monitoring meaningful data will get you into profit a lot faster than tracking things that have no bearing at all.

Track those things that directly affect your profit. Make decisions accordingly. That's what you do with operating metrics. By using them, you will see trends and patterns. Stay with the ones that favor your profit picture and take corrective action on those that cause you loss or hinder your progress.

Monitor For Trends

Here's how recording the data can work for you. In the auto recycling industry it is rare for an owner to have more than one location. It is

Tool

Use operating metrics to track those things that directly affect your profit. Record the metric the same day each month. It's best done on the 1st to coincide with the financial statements.

extremely rare for an owner to have more than 4 or 5. Ron had 6 active locations when he sold to GreenLeaf, a subsidiary of Ford Motor Company. Friends and associates would often question how Ron did this, making statements such as "It must drive you crazy!" or "I can't control even one; how do you handle 6?"

Ron's reply was always positive because he knew exactly what was going on in the areas of his businesses that, if not managed well, would cause him losses. He monitored these things by using weekly spreadsheets showing the operating metrics, just as we're discussing in this chapter.

Every Friday Ron knew exactly how many cars his employees had dismantled that week at each location. Every Monday he knew exactly what advice to give his managers based on the numbers he had received on the previous Friday.

"There may not be any more than 4 or 5 items you're monitoring at any one time," he says. "Just get the data. These are what I call pulse points. I record them on mini-metric worksheets and think about the data over the weekend. Ask yourself what you or your employees can do to affect those numbers in a positive way. When this becomes a habit, you'll find it is a key management tool. Monitoring just a few operating metrics in this way every week can elevate you from normalcy to

Tool

Many owners try to micro-manage everything. This is a mistake that takes their time and focus away from the higher level, more important things that will make the real difference in the success of their business.

Tool

Monitoring operating metrics can lead to greater ease in managing larger operations. You want to record information that allows you to see what's happening at key points in your operation.

Tool

A pulse point can be as basic as your gross sales at the end of the month or it can be the number of board feet of lumber sold in one day. Pulse points are those figures that show you whether you are getting ahead or falling behind.

Tool

As one of Ron's friends once suggested, "Learn to run your company from 30,000 feet and let your managers manage from 2,000 feet."

significance in your industry."

Of course, you've got to monitor the right things and you've got to make corrective decisions accordingly to keep your operation headed toward profit. The bigger your business grows, the more important it will become for you to watch the "pulse points" that affect the "blood stream" or cash flow of your business.

Do you see by now how important it is to monitor the trends that result from your company's actions? If you don't see it yet, you will as we go into planning and the setting of goals in our next section.

Give A Sense Of Ownership

The trend is up. The trend is down. But what if there's no apparent motion one way or the other? What can you do? How do you set a goal that will cause a positive upward turn to any specific number you are monitoring?

By measuring the subtle aspects of your operation, you are holding the keys to positive action. If you never look at the operating metrics or if you just record them and put them in the drawer without thinking about cause and effect, you are subjecting your business to the ugly whims of outside forces. You won't change your situation until you pick up these keys and begin analyzing what's causing your operation to go nowhere.

We want to be clear here for your sake. The consistent use of operating metrics is one of the most important tools you'll develop in your desire to reach significant success.

Operating metrics are the way you measure what you should monitor in order to maintain an upward climb.

If you have a larger organization, have your managers provide their own set of operating metrics to you each Friday. Pay them bonuses when their metrics beneficially affect your profit goal.

Many corporations in America today pay their managers bonuses based on company profits. We believe this is a mistake. We pay our managers bonuses based on what we want them to achieve on our behalf. We pay our sales managers bonuses as they reach goals we set by monitoring the sales metrics. We pay our operating managers bonuses when they help us reach goals we set by monitoring operating metrics. We pay our production managers and employees bonuses based on production. We pay our delivery drivers bonuses based on delivery performance. This manner of paying out bonuses, we believe, helps our managers focus on those things that bring about the profits we all want and isolate portions of the business that aren't contributing to the company's success.

Profits are inherent when you monitor the

Tool

Pay bonuses to personnel based on what they achieve to your benefit. Paying bonuses on profits is too vague. By monitoring operating metrics, you'll soon discover the actions that benefit your company and what doesn't. Pay bonuses on action taken toward those beneficial things.

Tool

Managers will soon discover that keeping operating metrics for you will benefit them as well.

Tool

Devise ways to reward all your employees for their positive influence as tracked by operating metrics.

metrics of your business and make decisions accordingly. Profits are nearly guaranteed when everyone in your operation is focusing on his assigned metrics, putting in the work that will cause growth, playing his part.

Within 90 days of gathering your first set of metrics, you should be able to decide which employees can most positively affect your profits. They are the ones you should target for rewards. You'll also discover which employees or departments are the laggards.

Isn't that how a football team achieves significant success? Everybody on the team has something to do that's important to the outcome of the game.

If everyone is focused on the thing he should be doing and each player does his thing to the best of his ability and works to improve, the team has a much better chance of standing out in league play at the end of the season.

If you just tell everybody you'll hand out a percentage on the bottom line, they won't feel like they control it. This approach is too indirect, too conceptual. They won't relate to it. It won't make sense to them because, to them, it's not achievable. Under this form of management they have trouble understanding or believing their job actually influences the company's profits. They don't know where the bottom line is.

If you tell everybody you'll pay bonuses on

measurable positive efforts to increase your profit in their area of control, however, you've given them a sense of ownership toward which they can dedicate themselves, because your gain is their gain. It's something they can hold that's more than a wage.

In certain circumstances, you may gain something else as well from them: an intangible called "loyalty." Bonuses generally motivate. They don't always create loyalty. Loyalty comes partly from the trust and respect imparted through your actions. Not every owner or manager can impart loyalty. But loyalty in an employee goes a long, long way toward assisting you on the road to prosperity. A loyal employee will defend you or your company in front of disgruntled customers. Loyal employees can even turn unhappy customers around.

Just be aware that the distribution of profits can be troublesome in a small, closely held business because the owner may choose to drive a Mercedes or have some other personal item as a company expense.

Employees know that such flamboyancy affects the profit picture; so reward them for those things they do that affect the company in a positive way. Try to attach the rewards you give directly to the metrics you are monitoring. Your employee will find new drive and new energy in this kind of relationship to their job.

Tool

Profit sharing is not always effective as a reward for reaching goals. Bonuses paid on specific goals attainable within the job description of each employee are more tangible and often far more motivating toward work output.

Benchmark For Improvement

The use of benchmarks is an interesting technique few small business entrepreneurs really understand or utilize correctly. A benchmark is a mark, a goal or a threshold set by other businesses (or yourself) against which you pit your efforts. You can set them and your staff can help you determine them.

You use operating metrics in the management of your operation to benchmark your progress.

In the field of business, benchmarking helps you understand where you are in the competition. Any business person who wants to create and stay in business must realize he has to compete in order to stay in business. Benchmarking helps that person compete more effectively!

Tool

Measure sales metrics on a per day basis. Sales relate directly to goals; so watching sales daily helps your salesmen meet weekly or monthly goals.

Certainly you will want to benchmark against the achievements of your competitors but you should also benchmark your progress against your current level of achievement. Sales should be monitored and thought about in daily terms, not monthly. Months have different numbers of days. If the selling month has three less days than the prior month and you are monitoring sales from a monthly point of view, you're going to conclude that sales that month were off and that conclusion may be quite erroneous.

This kind of benchmark awareness comes into play in budgeting. Almost everyone budgets on a monthly basis, but there's a mistake in that. It's better to go daily or weekly. If you are budgeting on a monthly basis, you set yourself up for misconceptions resulting from differences in the number of paydays from one month to the next. What's true for workdays is true for other costs as well. Those who are setting budgets from monthly numbers are operating under the potential of misconception and are not likely to monitor trends as effectively as those who manage daily or weekly.

Many important operating metrics cannot be measured in daily terms, however, and must be analyzed on a monthly basis. You've got to determine for yourself where the metric can be measured most effectively.

Benchmarking will help you determine this. Benchmarking is the act of measuring your progress. You can benchmark your company against other companies. You can benchmark against your peers, and you can benchmark against yourself.

Significant achievers do all three. These are the true competitors. They're always measuring their activities against the achievements of others. They've got a vision of standing out in front of their whole industry, and so they are benchmarking their progress by measuring it against all others who seem to be reaching for the same thing.

Monitor Your Operation

If you have several products or services bringing revenue into your business, which one or ones are the most profitable?

It's amazing how many business operators seem to ignore this basic question. If one aspect creates a profit picture faster and better than another, why do the other?

The answer to the question of what contributes the most to your wealth or what will bring it on most rapidly is so important that we can't ignore it here. If you do what you've always done, you will have the same results you've always had. That's a general theme among many businesses today. It's true whether you are operating a home-based business or a major corporation. To determine the correct answer, the one that leads you toward significant success, you have to study and perhaps discover what is most profitable to you and do that-and only that or more of that!

If some aspect of your operation is draining your resources, attack it. Your newly established habit of monitoring metrics will open your eyes. Once your eyes are open, you'll be able to see those things that are holding you back as well

Action!

Analyze your products and services to determine which are the most profitable.

Tool

You may have to gather metrics for your products and services separately in order to understand the real winners and the real losers of your product line.

as those that can escalate your enterprise into more profitable realms.

Know Your Business

In the early '90s, an auto recycler specialized in parts for early Mustangs. He focused primarily on those manufactured from '64 to '67. There were a lot of Mustangs being restored at the time.

His problem was not evident because he let his passion rule. He had a fixed and diminishing number of customers because every time someone restored a Mustang there was one less to be repaired. Ford wasn't making any more. Besides, there were several other outlets selling Mustang parts in his area.

This man was evidently blind to the floor on his market. He failed to plan any migration toward a more sustaining specialty. His business held intact for awhile, but then the bottom dropped out. He ran into financial trouble and had to borrow to stay alive. Later he developed another product line but still held on to selling Mustang parts. He could have avoided the costly near-death of his business had he analyzed the numbers on a continuing basis.

You have to know your business. You have to see from where your future business is going to come. You do this by watching the trends. In

Tool

Knowing your business means you have to devise ways to see ahead into the unfolding future of your operation, so that you can steer successfully through troublesome times.

this case, and it's true for many industries, there was a depleting finite number of customers to whom the gentleman had to sell. He let his passion rule, never considered that the number of buyers was diminishing all the time-until it was too late.

That's a classic example of going downhill when you should be looking for ways to go up. So when you're using metrics to measure your steps, consider some way of looking at the market trends as well. It should be obvious. Make sure you're not letting your passions rule your business behavior. Keep your eyes open to the marketplace. Know your customer.

Develop Your Expertise

You should also work at what you know and do best. Over the years, both Ron and DL had a lot of people suggest a number of good ideas. Ideas are plentiful. Accomplishment is not.

Ideas coming toward them were numerous. People suggested they start a paint shop, go into sheet metal, install windshields or set up a mechanical shop. But you have to control some aspect of your market before you take on new side trails. Most of these ideas would have led them down expensive paths of learning and start-up costs.

How many small business owners have you known who dabbled in a little of everything and didn't do much of anything right? How many have you known who had multiple business ventures but weren't seemingly successful at most or all of them? The problem is they are spreading themselves and their people too thin. They are not focused. They are not staying with that singular profession they do best. They are not working on improving what they do best because they are too busy trying new ideas and venturing down expensive sidetracks. These people will never reach the top of the hill. They will never know significant success because they constantly spread their energies and resources out to the point of ineffectiveness.

Tool

The best way to add new products or services is to analyze their true cost to you before offering them to your customers.

The best advice is to stay with what you know and improve on it. How does your customer view you? Upon what have you built the best part of your reputation? These are questions whose answers point to success.

Just because you see opportunity in a market doesn't mean you should go after it. It may not be your expertise. It may cost you your business trying to open up that opportunity. Do what you do best and improve upon it all the time. One day your competitors will not be able to keep up because you will have gotten out in front of them by being focused.

Also, don't undertake tasks you don't enjoy. Your success at these things will only be limited.

If it's a required task and must be done, consider delegating it.

Understand Your Core Competency

This is all about understanding not only what you do best, but also what you don't do best. You want to leverage your best efforts into something more. If you know what you don't do well and you need that function in your business in order to go to the next level, you can hire it.

Have a meeting with your employees in which together you define your core competencies.

Don't try to do something at which you are not good. Stay focused on what you do best. You're wasting your valuable time otherwise and probably costing yourself a lot of money.

Very successful people are generally very focused people who know how to delegate those things they do not do well.

In managing your company, you might look at it this way. Get everyone together. Ask them, "Okay, what are the things that we have to do in our day-to-day business? What's absolutely essential?"

For auto recyclers the answers are buying, dismantling, selling and delivering. You're looking for general categories. These "core competencies" must be defined for your industry.

Don't make the mistake of setting

benchmarks on yourself when you are defining your core competencies. Fed-Ex, for example, is *the* benchmark for delivery service. They are the ones who set the pace for on-time, prompt, courteous delivery, day after day.

Then the auto recyclers took the four categories of buying, dismantling, selling and delivering and defined their ultimate benchmark for each one. Dismantling was the only category found to be industry-specific; so they looked for a competitor against which to benchmark. Depending on the industry, you may find other considerations in your search for core competencies.

Once you have labeled those things you want to examine with your team, you look for a benchmark that will challenge you into doing better what you think you already do well. That benchmark is your target. Regardless of the industry in which you're involved, you should identify that benchmark appropriate to you and work to be better than that. Getting ahead of the benchmark is what this form of competition is all about.

Now you can look for ways to improve your core competency in that area. You can hire consultants, read books, attend seminars, talk to others, analyze the techniques you see your benchmark using. You can even mimic your benchmark as best you can until you figure out how that other company does what they do so

Tool

One way to go beyond your selected benchmarks is to understand what your competition is doing until you find weaknesses in their way of operating. Remind yourself that you want to be better or you'll only reach their level and will never go beyond.

well. Then you strive to improve upon it. You want to become the benchmark for someone else and hopefully even displace the benchmark company you picked in your brainstorm meeting.

Understand why they are better. Then try to get where they are and go beyond them.

Once you've taken this serious look at your core competencies and you've picked your model benchmarks, you are ready to go up against the two or three biggest competitors in your industry.

Remember, we're looking for the signpost at the top of the hill, the one pointing the way to significant success. If you are going to reach that distant place, you are going to have to go past your biggest competitors.

Be grueling in this analysis. You have defined your core competency in a certain area. You should then establish a benchmark by which you can measure your improvements. You must rate your operation honestly against your competitors when considering these core competencies. Otherwise you are lying to yourself, and that won't do you any good.

"In our own effort," Ron explained, "we had four columns, one under each core competency. In these columns we listed the names of those we determined as our top three competitors. They weren't always the same competitor depending on which column we were considering. For example, we decided another company, Troy's Foreign Car, was the number one for delivery, whipping us in service every day.

"Troy set the pace; so Troy became our target. Whatever they did regarding delivery service, we endeavored to do better. We honed our delivery service to our customers and theirs as well until we knew the general chatter about us was that we gave better service!"

You see? That's how you compete. You have to take aim. You have to see your target. You can't just shoot blindly from the hip. If you are going to be number one, know who's out in front and learn how they do business. Know their business better than they do and yours will sail out in front.

"It's worth mentioning," Ron added, "that in two of the columns, we believed we were the best. That meant that we only had to focus on the two where we were not. You might find the same. That didn't mean we could be lax in those areas. It meant that we should focus our improvement efforts on the two core areas where our competency level was perceivably behind a competitor."

Be Your Competitor's Customer

Here's another example of how you can improve yourself and your company. In one

Tool

Remember, you are competing with your selected benchmark; so don't go up against companies bigger than your goals and methods allow, at least not until you've grown to where you can actually compete with them.

instance, we surveyed our top one hundred customers, those who were most loyal and consistent in their buying from us.

We asked them all the same questions. These were the full gamut of questions concerning what they thought about the way we greeted customers, delivery times, the condition of parts they received. We wanted to see how they perceived us because we wanted to improve on our relationships with them. We figured if we could improve by the value of their feedback, then we could attract more customers into the same kind of loyalty.

We tallied the responses. One of the questions was, "Where do you shop when you don't come to us?" (We wanted to know who our number one competitor was in their eyes.) Three names came up routinely during this tally. There were others, but these three competitors showed up on the tally sheet quite often.

Once we knew who the competitors were in the eyes of our customers, we went to those competitors and, where we could, we took photos of their operation. We sat in their lobbies and talked with their customers. We talked to their employees whenever possible. We didn't tell them why we were there. Some of them may have recognized us, but that didn't matter. In essence we looked just like another customer.

We also took pictures of our own operation so that when we met with our managers, we

Tool

Don't be shy about going into the businesses of your competitors. Your purpose is to compare your way of operating with theirs. You may be surprised at the good ideas you'll pick up.

could compare ours with our competitors. This was a great discovery in visual cues. But the greatest breakthrough came from talking with the employees of our competitors. Now these people did not know who we were. We were discreet about it. But the information gathered from idle talk with competitors' employees and customers was very revealing.

We sat down with our managers and compared our operation with the others. We could all see the differences, which in some cases were quite obvious. We not only learned good things about our competitors; we also discovered their weaknesses! We now had targets we could all understand, and it helped us set specific and realistic goals that ended up bringing about the improvements we needed to get to the next level.

We want to emphasize that when considering your core competencies, you want to examine not only what you do well but also what your competition does well. That's how you're going to set your benchmarks. If you were a military leader going up against another army, wouldn't you want to know as much about that army as you possibly could? It should be no different for you in business with the exception that you're not out to decimate your competition, just get better than they are.

Action!

Decide who your most credible competitors are and analyze their operations relative to yours for things you can improve.

Big Problems First

How many companies spend a lot of employee time working on little things while overlooking the big problems? We believe you should always focus on the big problems first and work your way down to the efficiency of handling little problems once the big ones are out of the way. Big problems are easy to see, easy to get at and, quite often, easy to solve.

Domestic car manufacturers are still working on getting their defects per hundred down. This is one of their benchmarks. The Japanese are no longer working on parts per hundred. They are working on the way the radio knobs feel.

The Japanese are five years ahead of the domestic OEMs. They're working on the way the glove box opens and closes because they've done some studies that showed new car buyers are attracted to the luxury feel; so they built little shock absorbers into the closing mechanism of their glove boxes.

Our point is that you should work on the big problems first, and then work on the little problems. Your competitors most likely are not focused on solving the big problems. So if you work on the big ones first and then turn your attention to the little ones, you'll be out in front.

Tool

Identify the number one problem that reduces your gross sales or increases your expenses. Focus immediately on correcting this problem.

Analyze The Details

DL entered into his family's salvage business under what seemed to him a heavy hand. Among other tasks, he had to provide the statistics that would prove the purchasing numbers to his dad. He had to explain to his father "why" the company's averages were up or down.

"As a consequence," DL explained, "we ended up breaking out repairable vehicles from salvage vehicles, separating things out so that we could explain to ourselves how we were buying. As I grew more into my management position with the company, it became my responsibility at the end of the month to present the overall profit and loss statement to our management crew. Later we gave this job to an accountant, but at that time it was my job. I would ask the managers to explain the numbers for each branch of our business. Dad was absolutely persistent in his monthly pursuit to understand why there was any discrepancy between our planned budget and the actual numbers. He wanted to know why and would insist on knowing. My budget had to be within a couple of dollars."

DL continued, "That used to frustrate me until we caught a duplicate payment. We'd paid an employee tax twice. It first showed up on

Tool

A good plan forces accountability and creates expectations. It also provides internal benchmarks and milestones by which you can measure your progress.

Tool

A complete plan includes your financial goals and incorporates the use of operating metrics.

one month's profit and loss statement as double what the budget allowed. I learned a powerful lesson from Dad's insistence. I now understood that detailed care in monitoring the financials and metrics was very important to managing our business toward profit. This lesson was an essential part of my training new managers. It became a goal to instill upon them the importance of knowing where each portion of every sales dollar went."

Every dollar saved is a dollar added to your gross profit. You should throw your nickels around as though they're manhole covers! In other words, be a penny pincher. Details like these determine the difference between profit and loss.

Chapter 2

Get Ready; Get Set....

Why can't we just go? Why can't we just move forward on an idea? Why do we need to plan?

Do you load, shoot and then aim?

Joe goes into business for the first time. He has a good idea, capitalizes his business and thinks he can make it happen. Three-quarters of a year down the road, he's broke or floundering and wondering where all the money went. What went wrong?

Why do we need to plan?

Because you shoot after you take aim!

It's a question few ask in the beginning. People tend to run on what seems to be a good idea. They're running on emotion, however, if they don't plan. Planning is really a road map. Without it, you can get lost in the woods. We see it all the time. Too few business owners plan their operational activities. Either they don't understand the importance of good planning or they just don't know how to plan.

Action!

Schedule time to sit down and create an operating and financial plan for the next 12 months.

Planning is long-term thinking. It's a detailed look into what lies ahead. Good planning is a major contributor to company growth. It's a combination of management technique and due diligence. DL firmly believes it's one of the primary reasons his family business has enjoyed continued growth for four generations.

From DL's point of view, his grandfather, Don Fitzpatrick, Sr., was an excellent long-term thinker. DL's father, Don Fitzpatrick, Jr., saw this value in Fitz, Sr., as he grew into the shoes of the business. Having this role model and seeing the value in it, he worked to develop his own habit of planning.

As DL committed himself to the family business, he began to see the true value of planning. Perhaps it was just in his blood. Regardless, he entered every aspect of responsibility with a plan in hand. He knew it would not only benefit him, but the family business as well, because he grew up with the notion that planning is essential.

For DL, one plan was not enough. Each year he completed paperwork on three. The first addressed the activities and projections for the year to come. The second projected activities and schedules ahead three years by laying out goals highlighting major priorities to be met within that time span. The third plan generated by DL each year was a re-consideration and redrafting of a five-year plan.

"I always began the planning process in October by compiling notes and reviewing appropriate files I had collected over the year," explained DL.

An in-depth review of his budget requirements was also undertaken at that time.

By November, he would have the plan in a draft form, which he then passed out to key employees in the business as well as to his still active family members.

"Giving this draft to everyone in early November," DL said, "gave them time to think about my projections. They were all expected to add to it or challenge my various points, because we wanted to rely on the plan and would. November was their time to have valuable input."

By December, he'd worked through their comments and could then draft the final version. He then set it into the company's financial system and operating metrics. When January rolled around bringing in the New Year, the whole Fitz team was "ready to rock." Everyone knew what was expected. They knew how their performance would be measured as well as that particular part of the plan for which they would be held accountable.

Tool

Take notes during the first 10 months of each year in preparation for your business plan the following year. In October, compile these notes into a rough draft of your plan. Make your corrections and detail your thinking in November. After your directors and managers review it, you'll have it ready in December to launch the next year.

Have A Written Plan

The world has millions of dreamers, millions of people with good ideas. Good ideas are plentiful in the marketplace, but how many are reaching their goals? Who's making these dreams happen?

When goals are not being reached, there is without question an inherent reason why. Usually, it's either poor planning or no planning.

Poor planning produces poor performance. It's the "Five P" system of management. Poor planning is planning in the head, planning without putting things down on paper or in a computer where weaknesses can be studied and corrected beforehand.

Without a written plan, pitfalls lure you like a mirage. You can walk all the way across the desert thinking you're headed toward cooling water and a refreshing drink, only to be sadly disappointed when you realize it's not there and never was.

Without a written plan, dreams are just imaginations and generally fail to bear fruit because you've given them no foundation in reality. If you don't write down your plan, how will you examine its viability or look for its weaknesses? Don't risk everything on an idea in your head. Get it down on paper where you can see it.

Poor planning produces something, to be sure, because you are moving on an idea. The result, however, is seldom what you really want.

You have to plan. And all good plans are either on paper or held virtually in a computer.

You have to get the plan out of your head, in front of your eyes. For that matter, you want it in front of your managers' eyes as well. Not only will you then see its flaws more clearly, but you will also more easily solicit valuable input from key employees or your board of directors. That's how you strengthen your approach.

Tool

Get the plan out of your head by putting it on paper where you can analyze it for weaknesses that can be corrected.

DL provides an example from his own experience. This is an area many people overlook. DL came into his company as a fourth-generation son. Might sound easy, but for DL it was no silver spoon. The fact was, his father would not allow him into management until he'd finished his education in business management.

"Coming out of school," he says, "I developed a plan of where I wanted to go in the company. It would have been really easy to be cubby-holed and just do the same job over and over, but I didn't want that kind of life. So I did what I learned at college: I wrote my plan out on paper. I was starting at the bottom, essentially, and I wanted to move through the different ranks to become an owner alongside the other stockholders. I knew I had to excel at each position in order to do that. I knew they wouldn't just hand it over to me. They weren't like that."

So he wrote out a plan. He got it out in front of him where he could see it on paper. He studied it, carried it around, and looked for ways to improve it.

"From the plan, I could see that in some areas I had to further my education in order to gain more credentials for promotion. Being the boss's kid, I had to prove my credibility; so I worked on that plan as if it were a true company asset."

He also increased his credibility and value to the company by going through the MBA program in the evenings, a task that took three years.

In this example, DL first set his sights when he created that first plan on paper. At any point along the way he could look at the plan and remind himself that he really wanted it to happen.

"I had to work hard for it. I had to endure. I had to put in more time than I might otherwise have done. But I succeeded because I had the plan. I didn't just inherit my family business; I earned it the old-fashioned way. I grew into it by proving myself worthy, and I did that by following a plan from the very beginning."

Had DL stepped into a cubbyhole of

comfort, he'd likely still be there. He wouldn't have gained the position that allowed him to be the primary negotiator in the sale of his family's business to a subsidiary of Ford Motor Company.

Once your plan is in hand and out of your mind, it can be improved, and should be. You should visit it often, checking for a measure on whether or not you are reaching your goals. That's called progress, and it generally leads to success.

Set Attainable Goals

Reviewing past actions and their results through critical analysis is one of the good habits DL developed for himself. His process was to review what he had previously accomplished as well as take a look at those items he'd failed to achieve in earlier plans.

Once you know what you want to achieve, where you want to go, you can begin establishing your path by setting goals that will get you there step by step.

Objectives are like milestones on the path to the goal. You determine your objectives by reflecting on your goals. If you're not setting goals and reaching them, you won't need a long-term plan. Those who don't set goals and don't have milestones or benchmarks seldom realize

Tool

Experience, by definition, teaches us what to do as a result of experimentation. Some of the most valuable lessons we learn are "what not to do."

the kind of success we're writing about here.

An easily overlooked benefit from this kind of planning shows up when you go to talk to your banker. Bankers make loan decisions primarily on your ability to pay back the loan successfully. They back their decision on your ability to pay by using your collateral. A detailed business plan lends insight into how you expect to achieve those numbers. Without a plan, you're relying solely on collateral.

The foundation of a banker's confidence in your idea is based on the goals you have on paper, what milestones you've set and the potential for review of those goals as you achieve them. Having it all laid out on paper makes the backups and the letters of credit easier to acquire and the loan process easier to execute.

Leave Your Comfort Zone

How do you set a goal? The average business entrepreneur knows he wants success, but success is not a goal; it's an assumption. Everyone working for himself wants to be successful.

A goal is specific. It is a measure of success. You might say, "I want this much success (in numbers) by such and such date." That's a goal.

Planning then comes into play when you sit down with others who have influence on

Action!

List some simple personal goals you want to achieve this year, as well as over the next 5 and 10 year periods.

your thinking; and systematically, realistically and pragmatically figure out the most efficient ways to reach those numbers.

Thinking about the goals you want to reach causes the necessary planning to take place. You can define your goals on your own. You can sit down and write them out on paper and troubleshoot whether you are being realistic or not. Once you've defined your goals clearly and they are rock-solid in your head, then you are ready to put them in front of others and discuss ways of getting there.

This is about forcing yourself out of the comfort zone where you never ask the important questions. Goal setting forces you into the battleground of asking very important business questions so that you can plan how you'll reach the solutions.

Look in the mirror. Ask yourself what you want. Ask when you want it. Specify the date.

Now explain how you intend to get there. Fold your arms and require an answer. That's goal setting and planning in a nutshell.

Why did you buy this book? Our objective is to present ideas that, if implemented, will help you reach your goals.

Tool

In addition to setting goals, set milestones. Some should be short-term, perhaps even daily. These are your stepping stones to reaching the goals.

Action!

Set a goal today for when you intend to have the information necessary to set a goal for gross sales next month.

Ask Specific Questions

There is a basic truth at work behind every

successful business. In almost every case, the person who started it knew what he wanted to achieve before he set out. You have to define your goals before you can plan how you're going to reach them.

The process for vitality in business is simple:

1) Set goals for yourself and others.
2) Write a plan for reaching them.
3) Take action on your plan.
4) Require accountability.
5) Review your results.

Tool

When you set goals ask the proverbial "who, what, when, why and where."
Who's responsible?
What's the goal?
Where are you headed?
Why are you going there?
When do you plan on reaching it?

How do you set goals? How do you go about planning your steps? How do you implement them? How do you review them so that you can measure improvement? Who's going to be responsible? How's it going to happen? When is it going to happen? Where? Why?

It's the old "5 Ws" thing: who, what, when, where, and why.

If you can't answer these questions in detail, you are not ready yet. This is important in delegating as well. You can't just say, "Let's do better." You have to give your people tangible, quantifiable goals when you delegate. If your people can't answer these questions specifically, you should send them back to the drawing board. You may have to do that several times. You may have to go back there yourself several times.

Set Your Mark

After you've set your goal and created your plan, be certain that what you have in your plan is measurable. You've got to quantify it. You have to measure your progress in numbers or you won't know if you are succeeding according to your plan.

Here's an example. Ron decided his company would do some "outgoing marketing" to increase his sales of auto parts.

One of his financial friends, Clint Georg, said, "You know, Ron, that's great. You come up with a hundred ideas and maybe only two of them stick, but those two are always humdingers. If one is not working, you're always taking action on another. But I want to know how you're going to measure success on this idea of 'outgoing marketing'? I also want to know how you are going to determine the milestones to that success before you spend a hundred thousand dollars and fold it because it didn't work."

"Well, I don't understand." Ron was stymied.

"Figure out who your customer is, Ron. Then figure out how many calls your salespeople are going to make to these customers every day. Have them write down when they get an order or when they get a lead.

Tool

Measuring your progress in numbers allows you to better see when you've reached a specific goal.

Leads are alright because we might figure out that a certain percentage of them convert to sales; so have them record leads as well," Clint advised.

So Ron came up with a number for the 90-day point. "Okay," he said. "At the end of the 90-day period, we will have achieved [this number]."

"Now," Clint advised, "I'm going to challenge you with this: Is it fair to say that if you start calling people today, your success won't be achieved in total on the 90th day?"

"That's a fair statement. It won't be."

"Is it fair to say that you probably want to achieve a third of your success in the first 30 days, and then a third at 60 days, and the balance at 90?"

"Yeah, that's probably true, but in the first 4 weeks our customers will probably be taken back a bit by the idea and our salespeople will be learning how to do this better."

He clarified, "I'm just asking you to set the milestone. If you think only 20% of the goal you've set will be done in the first 30 days, and that at the end of 60 days you'll be at 45% and will have achieved 100% by the 90th day, then fine. But you have to set interim goals in advance!" he emphasized. "If you don't, you're always justifying to yourself and others why you should continue for yet another month and you'll keep on spending money on the project."

Tool

Milestones must be outlined in advance so that you can see whether or not you are reaching your goal on time.

Ron saw his wisdom. So before he started the projection, he projected his sales force should realize at least 20% of the total in sales and leads by the end of the first 30-day mark.

To his surprise, they reached only 3% of the overall goal at the end of thirty days; so he scrapped the project. He figured he'd saved a minimum of 2 months of fruitless expenditures and wrong direction by taking his friend's advice.

Had he taken on this project in his usual pattern, shooting for the 90-day mark, he would have justified why his people needed to go another 3 months beyond the initial 90-day period. The consequence of that kind of mistake would have added more expense to his losses, yielding only a low probability of success.

Is Bigger Better?

A lot of companies in the auto recycling industry are being consolidated right now. We believe this is true for companies in other industries as well. In the salvage business, being bigger does not necessarily allow you to buy wrecked cars any cheaper. Getting bigger definitely increases your accounting and administrative costs; yet it may not add to your buying power or your profit picture. (The administrative and accounting costs might be decreased, however, with improvement in management information systems, if they are available.)

Insurance companies sell wrecked cars at auctions, and the little guys pay the same price as the big guys. So in our industry, consolidation has not reduced our single biggest cost. When properly executed, consolidation can yield benefits such as a reduction in expenses in some areas. One of the primary benefits realized from most consolidations is strength in brand. That means more effective marketing at reduced costs, by virtue of size. It also means building a brand that the customer trusts. Many times, however, the benefits that are hoped for don't materialize.

Don't be intimidated because you see consolidation happening in your industry. Those growing bigger through consolidation are not necessarily better off. To combat the effects of "big" competitors, many small businesses are uniting to create new, more powerful cartels.

Do what's right for you. Don't react to what others are doing. Sit down, plan, think and do what is right for you.

Ron had a friend whose company nearly went broke trying to get bigger. He's now vice-chairman of a billion dollar company. He told Ron, "If your business involves inventory in a material amount, and being bigger does not give you an advantage in the cost of your inventory,

Tool

Rather than being intimidated by a large competitor, consider joining forces with some of your immediate competitors.

there probably isn't any reason to be bigger."

When Ron realized his industry was being consolidated and that his company was already pretty big, he decided that in order to compete effectively he'd have to become more efficient, a little more diversified perhaps, and grow some more. To achieve that, he'd have to improve his capital structure as well as his overall operation.

So he created a stock offering, sold some equity and roundedup a lot more money with the plan to leverage it into creating a bigger and better business.

Not long after, GreenLeaf negotiated to buy him out. Consolidation caught up before he reached his goal, although he had reached a major milestone by completing a successful private stock offering. Consolidation, in this case, left Ron and his investors a tidy return on their investments.

Know Your Core Customer

In our observation, no more than 5% of the salvage yards in the United States have decided to profile their primary customer.

Are your core customers male or female? Are your primary customers garages or collision repair shops? Or are they retail customers? Or wholesale?

Failing to define your primary customers is

Tool

Define your core customer in writing. It's harder than you may think! But doing so forces you to really consider who the primary people are that support your business.

placing your own obstacle in front of success. Without this knowledge, your salvage yard is buying at random and storing junk that'll likely never sell. The same is true for most businesses in most industries. A profile of the primary customers is essential to success.

This is important because your product or inventory must match the buying needs and habits of your primary customer. The service and quality of products you provide must be commensurate with your customers' needs and expectations. If you don't look at a precise definition of your core customer, how are you going to understand and meet his needs?

Too often in the auto-salvage business we see owners and managers who live under the belief that they "buy wrecked cars and sell parts". They think that's their business. They mistakenly conclude that every person who drives a car past their business is a prospective customer.

Here's a silly but at least partially true story: Many years ago there were two large catalogue sales companies. One published a book an inch and a half thick every year and mailed it to nearly everyone in the United States. The other company decided that they wanted to appeal to an upper-income customer only. They decided to be more specific. They wanted upper income females. They got even more specific in their profile; they wanted only upper income

Tool

Your products and services must match the buying habits and meet the needs of your core customer.

females with dogs. Okay-we're fabricating that!

You know what? They succeeded. And the company that mailed that shotgun blast of expensive catalogues finally went under.

Let's look at the floral industry for another example. How many florists conclude, "We buy plants; we sell plants", or "We buy flowers; we sell flowers." With that, they might conclude that everyone is their customer. As in our industry, we suspect that 95% of the florists operating in the U.S. have never bothered to isolate and profile their actual buying customers. Consequently they spend oodles of money marketing to the general public rather than targeting their actual buyers.

Ask yourself the following questions: Who are your customers? What are they like? What race are they? What are their professions? What are their needs? What level of income do they have? In what part of town do they live?

Then ask yourself these additional questions: Am I the low cost provider? Am I the elite line? Am I providing what they really want?

Exceptionally successful people do this. They define their target market. They set their aim and shoot at a specific bird in the flock rather than the whole flock. Most of their competitors shoot at the whole flock.

"Who is my customer?" Every entrepreneur

Action!

Define your core customer in writing.

Tool

You define your core customer by asking yourself exacting questions about the people who come in or call for orders. You haven't done your work on this until it's down on paper.

in every business venture out there who wishes to succeed should ask that question every day he or she comes to work. Whether you are working on the Internet or selling flowers from a shop or selling used auto parts wholesale, you should ask yourself daily, "Who is my customer?" The definitions may change, however; don't settle into believing that once you've defined your customer you never have to think about it again.

After a time, you will begin to see the true importance of asking yourself this question because you will see that you are spending less money on fruitless advertising and more on advertising that brings real results. Because you made a habit of asking yourself this question, your customer base will increase. You'll have happier, more loyal customers than you did before. Incidentally, business specialists more often than not get a better price for their product or services than business generalists.

You've got to know who your primary customer is. The more specific you are, the better. You can catch the overflow of secondary customers all the time, but don't plan on them. Your primary customer is your most important customer; he is your mainstay. He's the reason you are in business.

Define Your Place

Do you consider your company to be a low-cost provider, a high-service provider or a total-value provider?

Tool

A friend of Ron's once told him, "You can't have service, quality and price all at the best level." His friend advised him to chose any two but didn't believe he could provide all three.

If you can't provide the best service at the best price with the highest quality among all your competitors, decide which two attributes you can accomplish.

Ron admits it was hard, "You can never have a Nieman Marcus quality with a K-Mart price. Some retailers pride themselves," he says, "on quality first, cost last, and are very successful. Nieman Marcus spent a lot of money to make ladies think of them when they want a fine silk scarf. Nieman Marcus is proud of the fact that they provide the finest silk scarves, and they don't pretend to be cheap. WalMart on the other hand is more of a total-value supplier, handling a little bit of everything with reasonable quality at competitive prices. You've got to ask yourself, where do you fit in? What kind of provider are you in the marketplace of your industry?"

Your answers are dependent on the definition of your core customer. You want to match quality, service and price to the proper customer. The rest is marketing.

Change When Change Is Necessary

Most every manager is guilty of keeping non-performing employees too long. Let's say, a branch of a certain company is drastically under-performing. Looking at all angles, the owner finally realizes the problem lies with his manager, in that he is not forceful enough with the employees. He does not require or inspire good performance from the employees of that branch. But the owner doesn't do anything about the situation; he lets it continue as it always was. At best, he might give his manager a pep talk. The owner is guilty of the same flaw found in the manager.

Eventually, the company is bought in a consolidation. The regional manager of the larger company reviews the manager's job and finds there are no goals in place. The regional manager sets new goals and institutes a course of action, but the employees are still not performing. The branch is just not making it.

Soon thereafter, the regional manager moves up and another manager takes over the under-performing branch. The same results come in again. This branch is not performing to the standard necessary to justify its expense of operation.

How do we isolate the problem? By setting up and monitoring operating metrics, we discover there's never been a way to measure performance in this branch. The branch continues to cost its parent company more than it's worth.

Change is not going to happen until aggressive action is taken.

Fitz went through the process of setting up goals and budgets. But for two consecutive years, the company did not measure up to the new standards. DL wasn't pleased with the performance; so he did a study to figure out what an acceptable return would be to stockholders on all the assets employed in the business.

Fitz turned a lot of dollars and had more than 100 employees at that time. Through the analysis, DL discovered that he could better justify the assets by breaking them up, leasing some out and re-arranging the balance. This brought in a much better return. DL had taken an aggressive, necessary action by going to smaller operations that produced higher returns. The result was maximized shareholder return.

This is an example of restructuring something that was not performing due to a failure to meet goals and budgets. DL discovered he simply had to restructure and take a little more conservative approach to reach higher returns.

By downsizing, he put up a new building

Tool

Nothing will change about your situation until you take aggressive action.

and leased two other Fitz buildings to other proprietors. This allowed him to move more quickly into profitability to the benefit of his shareholders.

After all that, he instituted further measurable criteria for the following year. It would take awhile to know whether his directional shift was right or not. But the result was good. Fitz had one of the more profitable years they'd had in over a decade.

That put Fitz in a great position for the sale that came their way. The company looked a lot better than they would have had DL and his Board of Directors not taken these aggressive measures. That meant, of course, that their position in the negotiation was a lot stronger than it might have been otherwise.

"We took action on what we thought was best," DL explained. "We had no way of knowing at that point that the sale of our company was imminent."

Had DL not taken a financial look at their goals, he would have remained in a weaker position with the larger company. Had Fitz not admitted to themselves they were failing to reach achievable goals, they would have been dogging failure when the larger company made its approach.

It was a profound lesson in the principles of sound management, especially for DL. Had he not acted on an aggressive course of action when

Tool

Look at the assets listed on your balance sheet and consider the profit or loss you made last year. The degree of profit or loss helps you determine your return on those assets. It's a good number by which to measure your progress.

he first realized their goals were not being met, they might never have sold the company.

That's the value of setting measurable goals and of taking action when you need to take it. You always have a choice.

Weigh Cost Against Benefit

One of the biggest mistakes made by numerous small companies and many large corporations is the failure to make a cost-benefit analysis.

Before you make an acquisition or even take on a new product or offer a new service, you've got to do a cost-benefit analysis. You've got to determine what's there (in the enterprise you're looking to acquire or add on) and what it's going to cost you to make it reach the standard of performance where profit is realized.

You reflect that in the price. Cost is always part of the price. Just looking at the immediate price of an acquisition is a mistake. Its true cost includes what it's going to cost you to get the acquisition up and running into a profitable operation.

Failure to perform a scrutinizing cost-benefit analysis is one of the more common mistakes made as companies grow larger.

If your goal is to increase production or to accomplish more deliveries, you should

Tool

Anytime you acquire anything in business, you must consider what it is going to cost in order to get it up and running profitably. If the cost is too great, you shouldn't make the acquisition.

consider at least three factors that can affect the reaching of your goal. Determine the benefit of the goal to you; determine its potential benefits to your customers if you achieve it; and consider the cost of making the changes necessary to achieve it.

If the cost exceeds the benefits, you know you shouldn't undertake the initiative or acquisition. You are operating on ego, or a dream. So don't do it. Your desire could swamp you or cost you years of progress.

Cost-benefit analysis is one of the most important steering mechanisms you can employ as your company grows.

We all mull these things over in our heads. Rare is the manager or owner who records and examines the actual data on how many miles the truck has gone and projects from that data how far the truck will go and how much the fuel will cost. Rare is the one who will exact how much the driver costs and how many additional deliveries can come through re-routing.

Cost-benefit analysis weighs the costs against the benefits in order to see ahead whether a decision, action or acquisition will be profitable or not.

Those who do this are the ones in the 5% standout category. The rest are normal, falling into the 95% bracket.

Tool

Cost-benefit analysis measures the true cost of an acquisition against the benefits you hope it will bring. In this way, you weigh the validity of the purchase before you spend the money.

An Important Key

Anytime you are soliciting a bid for services or thinking about buying products from a new vendor, you should go through this process. The best way to go about this is submitting a Request For Proposal (RFP) to the new vendor or service provider.

Submitting a Request For Proposal forces you to write out a precise definition of what you are seeking. Oftentimes, this act of clarification stops you before you make a foolish commitment or contract. By putting your goal on paper, you may discover before you go to the vendor or service provider that your idea for a better "this or that" is just not worth it.

Action!

Use an RFP the next time you need a new service.

One of three things will happen. Either you can't define your objective, or you define it so well that your idea is overwhelming and you see that you can't do it (at that time), or you define it in such a way that your definition in itself becomes a valuable tool for reaching your goals.

Remember, RFPs relate to goal setting. You use RFPs to determine in advance whether an idea of yours is going to help you reach your goals (the ones you wrote down earlier).

One great characteristic of using written RFPs is their value to all parties concerned. You can hand them around to your board members, mentors and advisors before you hand them to the prospective vendor or service provider. Some very good feedback often comes back to you at this point.

But you'll see that good feedback comes back from your vendors and service providers as well. It's very important to clear the air up front in any business agreement. Your RFPs will state what you expect and give them a chance to state whether or not they can deliver on your expectation.

You'll never get that kind of feedback without a written document. The use of RFPs is a critical tool in your attaining significant success.

Use A PDA

Action!

Buy a PDA today.

Buy a PDA (Personal Digital Assistant) and carry it in your pocket if you expect to be successful from an organizational point of view. For this reason, Ron requires all his employees to have a pocket on their shirts! His managers carry a PDA and the other employees carry a pocket notepad while at work. The same is true for those who network in their business. Success is dependent on organization and being able to recall detailed information about someone or some event on the spot.

A PDA allows you to set goals in the

moment and recall them for examination later. You can easily compile notes stored in your digital assistant. The busier you are, the more important this kind of note storage becomes. You may think of something important while driving down the freeway, in heavy traffic (just don't enter it while driving). You may think of worthy ideas while waiting to be served at lunch. Having a digital assistant allows you great freedom to pick up and store these thoughts for later use, some of which could make all the difference in your planning or the attainment of your goals.

Once you start using a PDA, you will also find that it frees you up from the heavy "mind load" you've been used to carrying. You'll be happier, less stressed. You'll make better decisions, too, because your mind will be free to better discern.

You may not keep all the notes you take, but you will at least be able to examine them in more detail and compare different ideas you've had or suggestions people have given you. So you weed out the lesser and pull forward the more useful ideas. That's how truly productive managers get so many things done.

Planning is a conscious, routine effort that plays a daily role in your life. We hope you catch that. Using a PDA is taking advantage of the current technology in the most efficient way. With good notes filed where you can access

Tool

The PDA allows you to record any and all notes important to your planning as you go along. You compile them in October so you can finish your next year's plan by December of each year.

them as reminders, you'll find that planning is a snap.

Ron attributes a lot of his overall success to his use of a PDA, because it allows him to be more thorough. Friends and family members often call him for a phone number because they know he has it recorded in his PDA. If you ever meet Ron, he will likely ask you for a card. If there's even the most remote chance he can expect to network with you in anyway, he'll record your information in his PDA.

Here's a tip he'd like to pass along regarding the use of the calendar and address book: "This function is extremely valuable as it allows you to plan ahead months, even years. You'll never miss another birthday or a meeting with your banker. This incredible tool gives you powerful networking opportunities by virtue of its ability to link you up in a moment's notice."

Ron downloaded his address file and sent postcards to all his friends and acquaintances just prior to our going to press with this book. More than a third of them ordered a copy and many passed the information along to others.

When he needs a special shelving unit or a certain piece of equipment, he has the information at hand on his PDA, at least the contact person's name, address and phone number. Furthermore, this information goes back 10 years!

A PDA also allows you to be effective no

Tool

Your PDA won't work for you if it's sitting on a shelf somewhere. Make a habit of carrying it on your person where it will become truly useful.

matter where you are. You can use the functions to remind yourself of important callbacks, meetings, memos, and numbers as well as to layout your schedule.

Don't underestimate the importance of such a tool in your business. It's not a luxury; it's essential to anyone who wants to improve his or her personal and business management.

Measuring Up

DL was trained to buy a vehicle at an auction as cheaply as he could. His his previous manager showed him how to bid on the car by only bidding its worth to Fitz.

"That doesn't mean you want to give away money," the manager explained. "If you know you can get it for less, then do that! But in situations where you don't know whether they've called other auto recyclers or not, be fair about it."

(It's common practice in our industry for insurance adjusters seeking bids for salvage to call a number of recyclers.)

As DL applied this principle, he discovered it brought hidden benefits many times over from multiple vendors.

Prior to learning this technique, DL often experienced sellers coming around saying so and so had bid a certain amount on a particular

Tool

Always consider the needs of your customers when selling. Don't try to get "the last dollar" from them. You should sell on value, not price. You can't be everything to everybody; so go for the things that will bring your customers back time and again.

vehicle or vehicles and "would you like to bid higher?" He was in the habit of turning them down.

Following his manager's advice, he found many of these sellers knew he was giving a fair price consistently and stopped their competitive bidding. They'd just come straight to DL and sell to him on his word rather than going to another looking for a better price. DL was bidding on what it was worth to Fitz.

This developed into a pattern where adjusters and vendors also soon sold product to Fitz at DL's stated price. They knew DL and his team were honest, fair and consistent in their offers; so it was more worthwhile to sell rather than seek higher offers.

Many involved in buy-sell negotiations think that their goal is to "steal the deal." But relationships are more important. Reputations are built on fairness. Everyone is in business to gain; so everyone should gain in a business transaction. That's fair. This principle returned dynamic results to DL and Fitz, time after time.

Tool

Your business plan doesn't have to be complicated. It can be as simple as a list of a few financial and personal goals. Regardless of how complex you choose to make it, it absolutely must be in writing!

Three Simple Steps

There are basically three steps involved in setting goals and planning. It's the detail within these three steps that determines whether or not your plan is useful.

First, you are going to establish clearly defined goals on paper or in a computer, outside your mind where you and others can look at them.

Then you are going to plan how you are going to reach each of those goals and milestones on time. A good plan looks at the reality of accomplishing these goals. You don't want to lie to yourself or others just to please them because then you are not going to reach your goals, and that leaves everyone wondering, "What good was all that planning?"

Then last, you want to implement your plan. This should be quite easy because your plan has considered the details ahead of time. All you have to do now is take the steps you've already thought out.

Might seem simple. Maybe it's too simple because so many would-be business entrepreneurs fail to accomplish these three steps. They walk into their dreams without a plan, without examining the reality of possible events, without ruthless examination of the necessary steps.

If you are one of the exceptions to the majority, you'll plan. You'll set goals. You'll plan how to reach them and then you will implement them. Do this and you are on your way to significant success because you'll be able to lead and guide others with the clarity and wisdom of your thinking

Tool

Remember, there are essentially only two kinds of goals: financial and operational.

Chapter 3

Know Your Banker

Before you can know your banker as we're suggesting, you've got to understand what a "good banker" is to your business.

A banker, generally speaking, is not a business advisor. You don't want to ask your banker whether you should have four delivery trucks or five. He is not interested in that end of your business. Your banker only wants to know how many delivery trucks YOU want and how you're going to pay for them. He wants to see your cash flow. His responsibility is to ensure you're going to pay back any money he lends you.

Be sure that you take your loan officer a complete package that truly represents your financial picture to date.

If you are vague, you won't get what you're after. You can't say, "Well, we've been thinking about adding on...and we'd like to borrow about $400,000." That's not what your banker wants to hear. He or she is a financial officer with a fiduciary responsibility. Give him numbers in your request. He wants to know what your collateral is going to be. He wants to know how the purchase is going to affect your cash flow. He wants you to bring him a detailed plan. He needs to see the documents.

You'll want to answer all the questions he's going to ask before he asks them. If you've done your homework and looked correctly at your good banker's responsibilities, you'll get a call back that says, without further questioning, you've got the loan.

Answer all the questions in advance and you will gain a tremendous amount of respect and credibility. These important intangibles are power in business. When you've gained your good banker's respect and therefore own credibility in his or her eyes, you'll generally be able to accomplish whatever you go after.

Remember, a good banker is one who causes you to do all your homework before you ever meet with him. The responsibility is really yours. Exercise due diligence and your banker will be the proverbial "good banker".

"In my first fifteen years in business, I'd take my banker two or three sheets of paper and tell him what I wanted. We'd go back and forth, back and forth for weeks working through all that he needed to know. His job required him to write a loan narrative to pass along to his people. He'd attach whatever information I

Tool

Think ahead about the questions your banker might ask and have the answers ready. Don't leave any possible question unanswered. It pays to do your homework ahead of time.

brought.

"Don't misunderstand me. He was used to seeing sheets of paper and almost nothing else from most customers. But most customers don't get what they want. If you really want to be successful, make your banker's job easy. Take him what he needs to see to make a clear decision. Answer all his questions ahead of time. Working through this detail, working through the plan before you ever take it to your banker will always reveal weaknesses that you can either correct in the narrative or correct in the financials."

The best banker Ron ever had, he says, was a man named Jim Murray. "Jim did something no other banker has ever done. Anytime I went to meet with him, he got up and came around in front of his desk to meet with me at a small table in his office. It was very gracious and always made me feel like he truly wanted us to have a favorable banking relationship. The worst thing a banker ever said to me was a rather cold excuse, 'the folks with the gold make the rules!' That wasn't Jim."

Look for a gracious banker. They do exist and are not as rare as you might think. Let intuition be your guide. You're looking for a person with whom you can build an invaluable banking relationship.

Your best bet is to check around smaller to mid-size community banks. In this

Tool

Use the same graciousness Ron's banker showed by meeting with your employees on their side of your desk.

environment, you will stand a better chance of building a real relationship with a real person.

The biggest lending institutions have gone to "relationship bankers" for loans of less than $250,000. In these larger institutions, the "relationship banker" is really just a junior officer and likely has very little authority. They make loans solely on your credit score as generated from a computer data base, in conjunction, of course, with other underwriting criteria such as available collateral. In most of these larger institutions, the use of the title "relationship banker" is a misnomer.

You're much more likely to find a banking relationship with a small bank.

Five Things Bankers Check

Bankers must consider 5 basic criteria when analyzing your loan request. These are in no particular order.

1) Capacity

What is your capacity to repay the loan? Most banks won't support new business ventures if the sole ability to repay is based on projected returns. They must look for sources of repayment such as co-signers, sources of cash flow or additional collateral.

In the event you can't supply any additional collateral for your loan request, and have only projected numbers to go by, consider looking into a low doc SBA loan, but that would be for any request less than $150,000.

2) Credit

You won't get a loan with bad credit, not even an SBA loan. If you have weak credit or slow-pays, et cetera in your way, start today correcting that poor history. Then you may be eligible in about 12 months. Even one slow-pay can be a problem. Charge-offs or items sent for collection on low amounts are a big issue with bankers because they demonstrate your character and the risk they'd be taking if they granted your loan request. Many folks think small charge-offs won't hurt them, but all charge-offs are a big deal to bankers. If you have late payments on your home mortgage, that too is a big red flag!

Look at it from your banker's perspective. Anyone allowing small amounts to go for collection or failing to make mortgage payments in a timely manner will likely faulter on a commercial loan as well. That's how they see it, and that's why they'll deny your request. Good credit is very important.

3) Capital

Bankers expect you to have some skin in the game. Many would-be borrowers think the banks have the money, that they'll provide the money and you do the work. Wrong! The bank is a business too, and a regulated one at that.

Its officers won't make a loan for any amount more than 2 or 3 times the amount you put into your venture. This is the debt-to-equity ratio and it is an important consideration in the granting of loan requests.

4) Collateral

Collateral guarantees the banker there is something he can use to recoup the money should you default on the loan.

5) Character

This is similar to your credit report and certainly your credit report exemplifies your character. Many banks nowadays do background checks on borrowers, especially for higher loan amounts. They will call other customers in related businesses to ask about your character in your industry. That's why it's good to keep the alligators out of your pond the best you can. You don't want things cropping up that will destroy your chances of acquiring the funding you're seeking.

Most bankers today have software programs to assist them in analyzing your financials for variances, both good and bad. These programs even generate questions the banker should ask his customers who make a loan request. For example, "Why did the inventory grow 35% even though sales increased by only 20%?" The software would isolate the exact figures for him.

Look over your statements carefully before you present them and try to have answers for questions like that. If you do, you are demonstrating that you have control over your business. Bankers like to see that.

Keep your banker informed about positive developments in your enterprise. This is the place to brag when good things happen. Send him clippings from press releases you've gotten published. (That's better than sending him the actual press release.) He will place these in your file, and if he moves on before you meet for a loan request, that information will remain behind.

One of the biggest pet peeves for bankers is the customer who can't, won't or doesn't for any reason furnish financial statements when requesting a loan.

Tool

The business plan you must build to meet your goals successfully will serve just as well for a loan request.

In the early days, Ron saw this as an intrusion, because he wasn't prepared. But he had to turn around and prepare them or he wasn't going to get the loan. Preparing both current and projected financials, he soon realized great benefits. He discovered that the more he spent time thinking about the numbers and how to improve them, analyzing what they actually meant, the better he got at managing his business. The benefit wasn't just in pleasing the banker. He also found that from then on he was able to provide the banker with the documentation he needed to process a loan request.

The customer who fails to provide these

important documents is a poor manager and the banker can see that. He'll be very reluctant to loan to someone who doesn't take the time to understand the numbers and what they mean.

Have A Backup

How do you know you have a good banker? He visits your operation once every two months or maybe quarterly, but no less. He does this not to surprise you but to show a distinct interest in the progress you're making on your business plan. He's working on building a reciprocal relationship that is not dependent on whether or not you have a loan outstanding.

You should also follow up with him. If you want a good banker, give him reason to grow in his relationship with you. Give him a taste of the accuracy of your dream, show him evidence that vesting money in your operation is a sound business decision on his part.

DL does the same thing when he goes to the bank for backing. The approach has proven its worthiness in helping Fitz advance in directions they wanted to go. Preparing a package to DL means giving the banker all the information up front.

Why should they have to ask you for anything? Provide them with everything they

Tool

If feasible, scale back your goals for a loan request so that you can exceed your banker's expectations. Just remember, your cash flow must exceed your projected new-loan payments!

need and you have prepared the ground for a positive answer.

When Fitz built the Graham operation in 1992, they had to borrow substantial money to do it. In order to do that, DL and his father walked their banker through everything from the initial marketing study to why they were taking on the new site in the first place. They showed the banker minutes from the planning meetings and how they arrived at their decisions. They painted a complete picture and left nothing un-addressed.

That banker knew everything they were anticipating. He understood why they were venturing and could see the real potential of their desire.

But here's why all that preparation turned out to be so vital: that banker left that bank one month prior to approval of the loan package.

"Receiving that loan was vital to the progress of our operation," DL explained. "It was so important that we had backed ourselves up by going to another banker simultaneously." DL gives the credit to his father, Don, "because dad's experience had taught him the value of that. He is an excellent relationship manager."

Having the backup proved to be key because the new guy didn't have them over a barrel, didn't have to ask them to prove it all over again. Fitz got the loan by the fact that their history was complete in the bank's file. There were no

Tool

Some bankers will tell you they want all your business, but it's to your benefit to develop at least two banking relationships as this will likely lower your costs. Remember, however, that having 100 banks in your pocket won't help at all if you have poor credit.

more questions to ask.

If Fitz had not gotten it from the first bank, they would surely have received it from their back-up bank.

Do your homework. Answer the questions before you see your banker. Answer them on paper with provable numbers. Then back yourself up with an alternative source.

Though your first banker may not know or ever learn about the backup, having the alternative in the bag sharpens your inquiry and keeps your first relationship honest.

Another Kind Of Backup

In another example, DL, feeding his passion for flying, wanted to build for leasing, six hangers side by side at a local airport. As DL approached the reality, he kept his banker informed. He told her why he wanted to do it, showed her the market potential and gave her progress reports as he neared closure.

He didn't really need the money but felt his banker should know what he was doing and why. If something bigger were to present itself, he'd have his narrative in place. Not only did he know for himself that invested money would return, but he'd demonstrated to her that any money he might borrow on a bigger deal would return safely.

It's another form of backup.

DL would send his banker an email high-lighting his progress every couple of weeks or so to keep her informed of the developments.

"Because she's an aggressive banker," he says, "and because I've kept her informed, she called to let me in on some paperwork that would increase my credit line substantially. I hadn't asked her for it. I wasn't expecting it, and it didn't cost me a dime. She was playing her end of the business relationship we'd established. Her input actually reduced the interest that would fall in place if I were to acquire a loan package. That's the sign of a good banker!"

Keep your banker informed and build that relationship. It will pay off.

Protect Your Credit

A banker once sadly admitted to Ron that he had business relationships with fewer than 5% of his customers. The only time he ever saw 95% of his customers, he said, was when they were over-drawn, wanted a loan or were on the exception list.

Protect your credit. Fifteen years prior to the writing of this book, Ron went to a furniture store to buy some furniture. He was making pretty good money by then, nothing like now, but doing well enough to think he could just go and get the furniture for his house. To his surprise and disappointment, they turned him down for the loan.

He was shocked. Their reason for turning down the loan was because he had a couple of "slow-pays" registered against his credit card.

The rock in the path was Ron's own negligence. He had always had the money to pay the credit cards on time but had not developed a method for doing so.

"My habit at that time was to just pile bills up on the corner of my desk." he explained. "I just don't like paying bills. Maybe it takes me off my focus, whatever. It wasn't that I didn't have the money; it was that I didn't pay the bills on time. Well, it cost me that day! I vowed right then I was not going to have any more slow-pays on my credit report. I took all my personal bills and put them in the hands of my bookkeeper at work. I said, 'Here's the checkbook. Pay my personal bills as well. I'll give them to you as they come in.' To this day, I still don't pay my own bills personally. I don't write checks. I have someone else do it for me. If you can't do it for some reason, have someone you trust do it. If they don't want to, or are not any better at it than you, hire someone to do it. But pay your bills on time."

Any reader might want to say, "Sure, Ron. That's great for you, but I don't have your

Tool

Even one "slow payment" hurts; several will cause you to be listed as a "B" customer as they indicate a problem to bankers.

Tool

Remember to delegate tasks you don't do very well. You build strength in your company by utilizing the talents and skills of others where you are weak.

Order a copy of your
credit report today.

money. I can't afford to have a bookkeeper pay my personal bills."

Ron's answer is clear, "I remember when we used to come to the wrecking yard on Sundays and work long enough to get grocery money and then return with three kids to our mobile home. Seriously! We would go down there and sell parts until we had enough money to go to the grocery store, whether we were there for an hour or four hours."

Don't conclude from this that every bill has to be paid on time. Find out which ones report whether you pay on time and pay those bills on time. Always pay your banker on time, but delay your utility bill, for instance, if you must delay something. This strategy will benefit you later.

If you have to weigh between paying a utility bill and a loan payment because you don't have enough for both that day, pay the loan payment first. Do the same with a credit card minimum payment because that's essentially a loan payment. The utility has to go through giving you a notice before it will report you or turn you off. The loan officer will report your slow-pay the minute you miss the due date.

So no matter where you start, your objective is to build your credit. You do this by being savvy, by building faith where faith gets reported. When you don't do this, it will trip you up later on. Start today. Find ways to get the important bills paid right on time; then find ways to get all your bills paid when they are due. Don't overlook your personal bills while favoring your business bills. When it comes to credit, assuming you are the owner of your business, personal and business pay patterns are viewed as one and the same.

Don't allow yourself to get on the exceptions list, which is maintained by your banker or lien holder. Being on the exceptions list can mean you are supposed to have insurance on the vehicle and you don't, or that you didn't pay a tax when it was due, or return a required document or have insufficient funds for checks. That's as bad as "slow-pay" when it comes to loans because it shows your willingness to jeopardize the security on a loan. Get on that list and you'll have a tough time funding what you want to fund through loans.

Don't beat your banker up too badly about interest rates either, especially in the early days of building your credit.

Think of it this way: you want your loan officer, when you walk into the bank, to point you out and say something like, "Now there's a guy who makes a lot of money for us and he's a good customer." You want him to come out and shake your hand.

That won't happen if the only time you ever see him is when you are overdrawn, want a loan, have gotten on his exceptions list, or when you beat him up over a half-point on the interest

Action!

Subscribe to a credit bureau alert service today so you'll know when your credit is accessed or when derogatory information has been reported.

rates when you want a loan. He will generally give you a fair interest rate. He wants your business. He wants you to pay back the loans he gives you. So try to put yourself in the banker's seat and see what you look like coming into the bank.

Always be positive with your banker. He needs to know about problems, but don't dwell on them. When you do mention problems or difficulties, include a solution in your conversation. Bankers don't like to hear excuses. If another customer in your industry says he's having a great month and you're not, then your banker is going to wonder why. He'll simply conclude your competitor is doing a better job at sales or in managment. Your banker knows that you, barring uncontrollable outside circumstances, make your business what it is. You can't fool him, but you can show him that you are creative, responsible and willing to do whatever you can to make a go of it.

Work on your presentation; do your homework; protect your credit and you will rise to a new standard among bankers. Once you begin to reach more significant areas of financial possibility, you'll see how important this handling of your credit image is.

Inform Your Public

Any time you have a blurb in a newsletter or win an association award or promote an employee, notify the business editor of your local paper. Whenever you're published in a positive light in the newspaper or in a magazine or newsletter, mail a clipping to your banker. A good banker will file it in your credit file. When you apply for that big loan, that credit file goes around to all those other officers. They will see those clippings and read them, and that positive information will help bolster your relationships.

Every small business owner needs an understanding of publicity, what it is and how to go about generating it. Good publicity is visibility in a positive light. It doesn't just happen to you. If you sit around and wait for publicity to come to your door, you'll be mighty disappointed. It will never show up.

Publicity is something you generate from all the positive, productive things that happen to you. Positive publicity is money in the bank. It will bring customers to you, and it will give those who have the power to influence your business the impression that they should have. It gives you credibility.

Positive publicity shows that you are doing something well. It demonstrates that your business is progressing. Positive publicity adds to your importance within the business

Tool

Never hesitate to toot your own horn and promote yourself or your business. It's the surest way to increase your customer base, because if no one hears or reads about you, how will they know you're there?

community, and it reminds your customers of your presence.

The Value Of Press Releases

Don't underestimate the value of press releases for your business. In fact, you should set a goal of issuing one monthly, no less than 6 times a year. It's easy and costs almost nothing.

Look for things to announce: new products, employee promotions, a new service you're offering, a business contribution or awards your business has won.

Action!

Set a goal and prepare a schedule to issue press releases every other month so that you send out six each year.

You can write your own press releases. Ron did; and as a result has been written up in many newspapers and trade journals, including Inc. Magazine!

"Writing my own press releases," he says, "has been a huge boon to my business." And it can be for yours. "Eventually, I found a source for writing press releases and recommend you try her. Marcia Yudkin specializes in helping people and businesses write press releases. She can be reached at 612-266-1613. You'll find her easy to deal with and very inexpensive, just a few hundred dollars. What kind of ad can you get for $200? One story placed in a newspaper is more cost effective than an ad."

For direct mailings, use Mircrosoft Word. Go to the labels section where you can create and save a template of the addresses of your chosen media. Don't forget to include your banker as a mark to receive your press releases. Include other media of interest as you discover magazines that might be appropriate to your industry, trade journals and even newsletters that may relate to your business, such as one put out by your association. Ron's media list grew to well over 400 in just a few years. When a press release is ready, he prints out a mailing list on labels, and they go in the mail in no time. The technology and services are available to make this important task easy.

The key to placing press releases successfully is to make them about the benefits to consumers or customers who subscribe to your target publication. It won't be published if it simply promotes your business. A good professional helper like Marcia Yudkin can help you see this and improve your placement numbers.

Ask The Question

You want to make the banker's job easier. We can't emphasize this enough. Before we learned to develop these valuable relationships, we would sometimes find ourselves talking to bank directors who didn't understand our business. Bank directors are those ominous people who sit on the board of the bank and make decisions that seem like life or death.

Why not ask when you sit down, "Are there any directors in your bank who might need to better understand my business?"

Basically, this is not rude at all. You shouldn't offend anyone. It's good sense. You are just letting them know that you want your approval to go through without undue hindrance.

Tool

Once you have your operation looking good, invite your loan officer along with a bank director over for a look at how you do business. But you better have the polish on first.

Rather than sit down cold with bank directors who don't know you or your business, ask your loan officer to invite one of the directors along for lunch. If you are credible and your place of business looks good, getting that director in for a tour is a well-placed step in the right direction. Hopefully, the one that comes will be the one with influence on the board. You might even mention that to your loan officer at the time of the invitation or ask him to bring along a director who doesn't yet understand your business. It's all about image and credibility. If you have a positive image and can provide proof that you are credible, then that director will assure the others. If not, you'll have a pain in the backside working against you every time you approach that bank. He's more apt to vote on your behalf and argue to sway the others if he's met you, shaken your hand and likes you just a little bit, than if you're just a piece of paper and another loan number.

Action

Take your banker to lunch.

Do your homework. Learn how to impress and remind with positive publicity. Keep your banker informed and take him to lunch every now and then. Try to understand his "buttons". Some are nuts about an exception; others are nuts about overdrafts. You'll want to try to perform on all counts related to bankers, but you really want to understand what's "deadly" in their view. Know that being overdrawn on the last day of the month puts you on the director's report. All in all, just learn how to make your banker's life easier and that person will do a lot for you.

Tool

Make your banker's life easier and he or she will do a lot more for you. Never, never allow yourself to be overdrawn at the end of the month!

Use Debt Wisely

The first few years in business, Ron showed very little income. Like a lot of small business owners, whenever there was enough cash, he'd pay himself more. Granted, he didn't have to pay much in income taxes during that time, but he didn't realize how it was all working against him until he went into the bank to borrow money for expansion.

Ron wanted $250,000 to put up a new building and buy some delivery trucks. The banker looked at his income tax statements and said, "But Ron, you only made $20,000 last year! The payments on this loan are over $50,000 a year! How could you possibly pay this loan back? You can't pay this loan. I can't give you this loan! I know you tell me you're making income; that's great. But you're going to have to show it on the tax returns. That's not to say that we don't understand that you are a small business entrepreneur, but you're going to have to show a lot more than $20,000 income before we can ever grant a loan of this magnitude."

That was a hard lesson! It included a little embarrassment. But then, that's the kind of thing you don't forget. What you do with it is the determining factor for your future. As for Ron, he changed the picture. He worked on understanding the banker's perspective. He troubled himself about learning to manage his money so that all the paperwork was there and his income was as accurately stated as feasible. It took awhile, but it made a significant difference in his business. Growth in his business was basically delayed because of his poor planning.

Chapter 4

Bank On It

Ron knew a businessman who accumulated more than $300,000 in cash over a 10-year period. He kept it in coffee cans! His statement to Ron was succinct.

"I was the most stupid guy, Ron, you could possibly imagine!"

Ron acquiesced and let him talk.

"As I got the money, if I had put it in the bank and paid the taxes, over a ten-year period that's only $30,000 a year in income; in a 20% tax bracket, that's $6,000 in taxes. I would have had $24,000 a year. If I'd bought one piece of real estate or more inventory or added onto my building, whatever...that $300,000 would have been a million in ten years. What did I have to show for it? $300,000."

"And you can't go spend it; can you?"

"No," the man confessed, "I have to dole it

Tool

Hiding money is like running a hose under the pavement of your driveway: sooner or later it will cave in.

out somehow." Not to mention that he'd put himself in position for constant worry about the IRS coming after him.

You know what? When you hide money as this man did, you can only safely spend what you can eat, what you can wear and what you can put in your home. If you're trying to hide more than that, you're in big trouble. It will show up sooner or later and you're really only cheating yourself.

It's a dangerous game to play.

Pay Your Taxes

There have to be advantages to owning your own business. There have to be. Ron had an accountant who told him and his two partners that all three couldn't buy new pickups unless they left them at the business at night.

"Now that's just silly," Ron said, recounting the time. "We all knew it was silly and we fired him. He didn't work for us anymore, and he drove home in an old pickup.

"We wanted to buy new pickups and we did. We used them every day in the business, and we understood what that accountant had told us. IRS code said that unless the truck was left at the business at night or you kept an exacting log, you could get in trouble. Well, the code is more generous now (at the time of this writing) than it was then."

The reality is that everybody buys a pickup at the business and takes it home. It's their vehicle. Examples like that show the advantages of ownership. Ownership looks to taking perks wherever it can.

The moral of these stories is a common theme. You have to show an accurate income picture. Why? It enables you to borrow money, to capitalize your business when you need to or want to move forward, and it keeps you out of trouble with the taxman.

That's the flip side of capitalism in America. Those who can borrow have the means to move forward. Those who establish and hold good credit are never hindered in their bid for progress.

Those who can't borrow because of bad credit ratings or slow-pays are in a fix. But there is a message here. If you are at the bottom, stuck in the mud of poor habits of management, start today. Start building your credit. It starts with being wise to how it works, wise to the advantages good credit and paying taxes can bring your way. Don't hide all your income; show it. Then use that showing to your advantage. Take it to the bank and borrow more of what you need in order to grow to an even better income. If you are forced to grow using only your own money, it will minimize the chances of your significant success.

You don't want to be foolish on the upside of paying taxes. Take advantage through a knowledgeable accountant of all the savings you can. But don't be foolish on the downside either by hoarding and hiding cash. You'll only dig a hole for yourself. Pay your due taxes and then turn around and use the evidence of that to grow your company to the point where you won't care so much about the tax money spent. You won't care when your income is sufficient to meet all your desires.

Compare The Returns

Tool

Focus on turns first; margins, second!

Inventory plays a role in generating income. One of Ron's good friends, Gary McKinney, a new car dealer, taught him to focus on turns first, margins last. If you are analyzing a return on something over a yearly basis and you put money into materials that return a 50% margin over the year and you compare that to inventory that turns over quickly at 20%, consider how much more you'd make if you turned the smaller margin over six times a year as opposed to the larger margin only once a year.

That's a quick look. You might stumble over it momentarily but if you slow down and think about what we're suggesting for even a moment, you'll walk away from reading this book with a much greater capacity to make money.

Hundreds of business owners fall into the trap of buying the big item or the pretty item with the money they've generated. Perhaps they think they look good to have it around. But if cash flow is thin, stay away from items that turn over slowly and favor the inventory that turns rapidly. You'll generate a whole lot more of that valuable revenue from items that, though they may have a smaller profit margin, are favorites among customers.

Now there's a calculable point of poor return for which you want to watch. Don't go by a blanket statement. Big margins are not bad and little margins that turn rapidly are not all favorable to your business profit. Get out your calculator and crunch some numbers. Be honest with yourself. Make judgments based on weighing percentages. You won't really know until you do the numbers crunching yourself.

At Fitz, DL and his father followed a profitable numbers trail toward acquiring more trucks for salvage because they observed that, though the margins were not as high as some of their other products, truck parts turned over rapidly. They could hardly keep them in their inventory.

"We'd buy them; money would flow like the snap of a finger, sometimes almost before we could process the parts through our system," DL said. "We learned by analyzing the

Tool

Many small business owners don't understand the importance of turns and never attempt to measure them. This is a bad mistake and one you want to avoid.

numbers. We made a very progressive buying decision by comparing returns."

Cash Trickle, Cash Flow

Let's make it jump off the page at you. If you didn't comprehend what we just told you, then look at it another way.

A man starts out in the floral business. He buys a dozen roses at wholesale. He pays $10 for them. He sells them for $30, making a 200% markup.

Tool

If you don't understand turns and how to measure them, set up a meeting with your accountant or financial advisor to learn how to understand and monitor this important business tool.

The numbers cruncher sees it in columns. In the first column, he paid $10. In the second column, he earned $30. In the third column, he wrote his gross margin entry of $20.

Now let's say this florist sells a dozen roses only once a month, for whatever reason. How much does he have at the end of the year?

If he made $20 per dozen and only sold one dozen each month, he made an annual return of $240 by reselling roses.

Across town, his competitor buys a similar dozen roses for the same amount. But this other florist might have a stronger customer base and may be a better marketer. He turns roses over at a greater rate; so he can give his customers a better price. He turns over a lot more roses in the dozens. At the end of the year, though he's made less on the margin, he's grossed more on the returns.

Does it pay to look at the numbers? You bet. Better do it. If you don't, you're walking through your business life with your head turned around backwards. Turn around and look where you're going. Look at what makes profit and focus on that. Stay away from products that turn over too slowly. Cash Flow is the name of the game.

Our second florist, let's say, is selling his dozen roses for only $20. That's 30% cheaper than his competitor. So more customers are coming to him for their roses. He's selling at the average of one dozen a week. But he makes only a 100% markup. In a year's time however, he does this 52 times as compared to the first florist who makes a 200% markup only 12 times a year.

We can readily see that the second florist makes the most money based on his turn-around figures. Instead of $240 for the year, he's generated $520 for the year.

Now that ought to grab your attention!

Although we're giving you a hypothetical situation with small numbers, you can easily see what understanding the numbers can mean to your business. You magnify numbers in the sheer quantity of inventory in relation to your customer base. Generally speaking, having more customers means having more opportunities to sell. This is especially true if

Tool

Numbers are the language that most accurately describes the unfolding trends in your business operation. It pays to study them, use them and to become good at it. Think metrics!

you are providing what they want at a price they're happy to pay.

If you don't crunch the numbers, if you don't analyze the returns, how will you ever know? You may be losing a ton of money. Maybe there's a way to generate more. Crunching the numbers will reveal this to you.

Focus on the turns; watch the margins and understand both.

True Cost

We are not advocating here that you be the low-cost provider. In some industries it might be the right thing to do, but not always. You want to understand your true cost.

Tool

You always want to calculate and understand the true cost of something before you make any decisions on pricing and stocking inventory.

Most business owners do not really understand their costs for inventory or services. They know that they buy tapes for a dollar and they sell them for two dollars, but they fail to understand that they have forty-six workers sorting them. They have cardboard in which to box them, and a host of other related costs. They know they have a hundred thousand a month in sales and that their tapes are only costing them fifty grand. They know they don't have any money in the bank, and they are not really sure why.

It's because they have made no effort to understand their true costs in buying, selling and distributing their products.

You must understand the true cost of your products before you make decisions on pricing or stocking of inventory. It's important that you understand your costs. Many business people don't.

Ask For Sales

The topic of sales is broad. It is so broad that, like the concept of "love", many people take it for granted and conclude they don't have to work at it. Sales just happen if you set up shop and have a product. Right? No. Don't take your sales for granted. Even if a certain amount of income comes almost automatically from walk-in sales that seem to happen whether you do anything or not, every business has the potential to increase its sales results.

Certainly you must match your product to your customer. You do that by defining your core customer as we discussed earlier. Creating increased sales is mostly science, not art. Salespeople are supposed to have this skill when they come to work for you, but not all of them possess it to the same degree. As a business owner, you should never rely totally on the skill level of salespeople who come into your organization. Learn from every one of them. Investigate on your own the elusive cause behind increased or decreased sales. Read everything you can about how to generate sales. Talk to others in your industry. Follow their advice wherever it may apply. Experiment and monitor your progress.

You increase sales first of all by monitoring the actual numbers. How will you know something is working if you don't have metrics against which to weigh your results?

The production output of your sales staff is directly related to their belief in you and your company. Give them reason to believe in you. Ask them what you can do to help them increase their sales. Provide them with ongoing sales training as you can afford it. As a manager, you are the goal setter as well. Set their goals realistically from the numbers you are monitoring and ask them what they think their goal should be. Then, as they reach those goals for you, reward them accordingly. When they don't reach those goals, talk to them about why they think they didn't. Maybe you weren't realistic. Maybe they didn't work hard enough; maybe someone is not asking for the sale.

If you are directly involved in customer sales, then you'll want to be aggressive on the floor or phone by learning to ask for the sale. This is a key ingredient to increasing sales. Never put your customer off for a future sale. Ask them if they are going to pay by credit card or check. Ask them when they would like to

Action!

Set sales goals for your company as well as separately for each sales person to project over the next 90 days.

have their purchase delivered. Always ask "closing" questions that can't be answered with a yes or no. How you do it is up to you, but don't let them go without asking for the sale.

Observing other businesses within the auto recycling industry as well as businesses in industries where we're the customers, we see that too few salespeople actually ask for the sale.

Become the customer and watch how other professionals with you. You should go do this for a week. We dare say that in at least 90% of the situations you encounter, the salesclerk or salesperson or business owner WILL NOT ask for the sale while you are right in front of them or on the phone.

What happens to a customer who walks away without committing? Watch what happens to you. Given time to think about it, you will likely talk yourself out of it. You will consider other alternatives or reconsider the price. You may just decide not to buy.

Make sure you and those on your staff are selling, not just going through the motions of this vital part of growing a successful business.

If your business has maintained a sustained period of non-growth, chances are realistic that you and your employees have fallen out of the habit of asking for the sale.

Tool

Train your salespeople to assume that the sale is going to happen with every customer. Teach yourself and your sales staff how to ask closing questions that customer's can't answer with a simple yes or no.

Action!

Schedule at least one sales-training class per month for the next 3 months.

The Incentive To Sell

What does "selling" mean to you? Have you thought about it much? Based on what you see in buyer/seller relationships in all industries related to your personal experience, we'd wager that most people have not thought much about it. To most people involved in selling, there is a unilateral assumption that it is simply a matter of being there, of being polite, and giving good service.

We believe selling is an active effort, not a passive one. You can be polite and still be aggressive. Our connotation here is that aggressiveness is related to action that takes place from thinking about, analyzing and monitoring results.

Ask yourself whether you're thinking about your sales or not? Are you looking at ways to improve them? Are you monitoring them at all? Can you monitor them better? Can you provide better motivation to your sales force so that they want to improve their sales?

There's a long list of questions like those above that you could ask yourself regarding sales in your business.

Let's look at an example from our hypothetical florist. Let's say that Joe hires a polite, courteous and knowledgeable woman named Martha to tend the counter and answer the phone. Joe pays Martha $400 a week to do this.

Would Martha make more sales for Joe if he paid her a base of $300 a week and a commission of 10% on all her sales?

He would certainly add motivation for Martha to sell. Does she have the skill and the tools to do better? Has she been trained in selling? Has Joe provided her with sales tools such as brochures and business cards? Is Joe providing ongoing training of any sort to keep Martha in the habit of believing she can sell and increase her knowledge of the science? Does he set goals that include her input? Has he established milestones? Does he monitor her progress daily? Does he keep her informed on her performance?

If Martha is given motivation or incentive to sell and assisted through training, she will sell more than she did before. But don't overlook the high degree of importance that, in order for Martha to really excel on behalf of Joe and his business, she's got to ask for the sale every time there's a customer in front of her or on the phone.

Action!

Set daily sales goals for each salesperson and integrate little ways to reward them for success in front of the others.

Use A Mystery Shopper

Ah! Now we're getting into advanced strategies in the science of increasing sales. Want to know more about how your salespeople are performing? Use a mystery shopper.

Most large cities have professional firms that specialize in this type of research. If you can't find one or feel their service is too expensive for your budget right now, ask a relative or friend to help.

Mystery shoppers look and sound like any anonymous customer who might walk in your door or call your business on the phone. But their motivation is different. They might buy or they might not. They want to see how your salespeople respond to their inquiry (and that might include you!).

This is the perfect way to determine whether you and your staff are asking for the sale each time.

Your mystery shopper will tell you valuable things such as how many times the phone rang before it was answered and whether or not the salesperson was courteous. Good ones will report the impression they had when they first came in the door. Were they greeted well? Were they recognized (as a customer)? Were they assisted within a reasonable time?

A mystery shopper is a hired investigator who on a minor level will reveal insight into how your operation is coming across to all customers. He or she will also inform you of areas where you and your sales staff need to apply some technique or go for further training.

Hiring a mystery shopper or two

Tool

To add objectivity to this strategy, create a series of items for your shopper to verify and tally the score on these items. This objectivity will allow you to benchmark the service of your employees one with another. All this helps you manage for improvements.

periodically will keep the bugs out of your sales and help ensure your progress toward significant success.

Ron used the results obtained from mystery shoppers objectively to track progress of new hires as well as the performance of all his salespeople. He prepared objective criteria for the shoppers and tabulated scores for his salespeople.

Now that you understand what a mystery shopper is in relation to your own business, turn the table around and send this same artisan to your competitors. A good mystery shopper will inform you of their habits, good and bad, just as well as he or she does your own. You might be surprised at what you learn. You'll learn two things for certain: what NOT to do and what to do BETTER.

Tool

By mystery shopping some of your competitors, you will discover many surprising things about them and it will help you glean valuable insights about your own operation.

Point Of Sale

Why would you ever want to go through all these things we've suggested in this chapter? Are these really important to significant success? Why can't we just start, go to work and expect that we'll come out ahead in the end?

It doesn't work that way.

If you sell products or services, everything in your business revolves around the point of sale. Certainly, we've demonstrated that getting that bank loan and moving ahead depends on what happens at your point of sale. We've also brought you chronologically to the point of sale, the foundation stone of success. We want you to realize how important it is to do all the research you can over the course of your business, especially regarding your success rate at sales and that of your sales team.

Obviously, you want to understand specifically what's happening at each point of sale in your business. Don't take this lightly. More importantly, you have to understand if there even is a point of sale!

Almost sounds silly, doesn't it? But if you could turn around the thousands of would-be customers who may walk out of your business someday or hang up the phone without ever buying from you, wouldn't you want to do so?

That's why you do the research. It's why you crunch the numbers, why you monitor sales metrics and set goals. It's why you ask for the sale every time. It's so that you CAN TURN THOSE WOULD-BE CUSTOMERS around.

Every detail of every aspect of our sales over the years has been examined and analyzed for improvement. We're encouraging you to do the same and showing you some of the steps we've learned to put into action. Just realize that once you lay this book down, you are out of our grasp. We can influence you only by what you remember.

Tool

Over time, you should examine every detail of every aspect of your sales, always analyzing for ways to improve the numbers.

As for us, we are just passing on our experiences as well as some of the principles we feel have led to the significance of our success. We hope you're reading carefully. You can't just sit by and wait for the orders to come in. You've got to be aggressive on every front.

Overcoming Roadblocks

Will you have obstacles in front of you? We don't hesitate for a moment to tell you that you already do. A very high percentage of small business start-ups fail in their first year of effort. If you are fortunate enough to survive your first three or four years, you will have already discovered the value of some of what we're giving you in these pages. But our goal is to take you a step further. We want you to succeed significantly.

We believe the ability to overcome obstacles is as much a mindset as it is a matter of developed habit. You fortify your mindset and strengthen your habits through training, discipline and management.

Pretend for the sake of illustration that training, discipline and management are passengers in your car. Your car is your business and you as owner are driving them down the avenue of success. As the driver, you set the speed. If you don't pay attention, you could

Tool

Fortify your ability to overcome obstacles by strengthening your business habits through training, self-discipline and good management.

crash.

What do you do when you meet an obstacle in the road? Do you panic? Quit? Turn around?

Or do you look for a way around the obstacle? You'll find that training, discipline and management can help you find your way around the obstacle.

Having read our book this far, few obstacles will surprise you because you're likely monitoring the warning signs.

Tool

Remember: the skill to overcome obstacles starts at the top of your management team and trickles down. If you're the owner, it starts with you!

Furthermore, few obstacles will stop you. You don't look at obstacles as solid things that can't be overcome or torn down. You are geared for success. You look for solutions.

The skill to overcome obstacles is not brought on board with an employee's credentials. It comes from the top down. Remember, you're the driver. Every one working for you will look to you when obstacles arise. Your employees can help you, but you are the influence.

Priceless stuff! Hope you're not missing it.

If your crew holds this respect, admiration and devotion toward you, your customers will also.

Why? Because your employees represent you at the point of sale!

A Stronger Business

If you have more than one salesperson, ask them to give you at least three ideas of what you (their company) can do to increase their sales. Point out that if their suggestions increase their individual sales, their income will increase as well.

Don't open up a Pandora's box with this. Limit this inquiry to three good answers from each salesperson or employee so that they will be more thoughtful about and specific with their answers. Require them to write them down, not just verbalize them.

Here are three good ideas that came back to Ron when he did this many years ago.

His operation had a key-phone system, the kind with buttons along the bottom for different lines, where a light goes on when a line is in use. An employee would have to shout, "Joe, line three!" or whatever, when a customer asked for a specific sales customer representative. The first good idea suggested was implemented almost immediately with the installation of a quality electronic phone system.

The second profit-making idea to come from Ron's employees was arranging to accept American Express credit cards, something he had not already done. "Most of our wholesale accounts pay with American Express because it's a business credit card. They don't pay with

Tool

Show your salespeople how an increase in their sales figures will directly increase their personal income. If you haven't yet set it up that way, you should do so as soon as possible.

Visa or Master Card, especially the larger accounts; so this idea made us a lot of money. Our business revenue went up almost immediately by $50,000 a month!"

The third suggestion that came into being from Ron's employees was a failure. It was to take on one of those programs that, for 3%, guaranteed a customer's check on a C.O.D. shipment. Ron's team soon learned that most customers were unwilling to pay the 3% service charge and that, if he was to absorb it, it would take too much away from his sales margin. Ron also tracked the number of C.O.D. sales before and after setting up the guaranteed check system and found that the sales did not go up following its installation. So that idea was a failure.

The first idea allowed something else. It added scalability to the sales floor. Sales increased because of the improved communications, and the increase allowed Ron to hire more sales staff.

Though the last idea did not work to increase sales, it did increase the employee's feeling of worth about Ron and his company. Asking the opinion of your employees brings them more into the picture of success. When they truly feel they are contributing, they will be more loyal. It's a win-win management technique. Besides, Ron didn't think of it, and it could have worked to serve a greater profit. Your employees are

Tool

The only way you'll really know whether or not sales are increasing is to monitor them through operating metrics. Numbers count. Numbers are your business. Start using them.

your representatives at the point of sale. They can bring back valuable information, ideas and experience you might otherwise overlook.

So keep your ears open to their voices. You'll build loyalty for certain and a stronger business as well. Both Ron's and DL's businesses have grown because they put a value on what their employees had to say.

Chapter 5

Internal Focus

Your core products or services are those on which you make the most money. If you focus on them, they become your specialty. People will learn soon enough they can readily fulfill their special interest or fill their need at your business.

Ron has three sons, all of whom have established auto-recycling facilities under varying degress of his mentoring. Two of them specialize in older-model import cars; and the other, in Jeep parts. It did not take long for owners of these brands to learn they could readily find needed parts at one of these facilities. Also, it didn't take long for his boys to become experts in their fields of specialty. It's more important to know everything about something than a little about everything.

Ron's sons generally get more for their parts than those competitors who dismantle every kind of car because his sons have become extremely knowledgeable about their specialty parts. Each has identified his core customer, matched his products and service to that customer, and focused his marketing accordingly. In each case, a particular brand is his core product. They sell other items, but they make the most on recycled products related to their brand specialty.

How do you decide what your core product is going to be? You might think it's a matter of simply going for your passion, but that's not the foundation for a good business decision.

The market demand for your core product must be there. You'll find it by watching trends, crunching numbers, and testing the market. You can also identify it by separating your metrics by product or service line. Intuitively, you probably know exactly what your core product is, but you may have drifted into lots of other initiatives. You want to get a good price consistently or you may find that offering a certain product is not worthwhile. Interest in and need for the product line of your choice has to be there, and you are going to want to feel confident that both the interest and the need are going to stay in the market for a long time.

You also want to make sure your supply for the core product will be available for you to build a business around it. Remember the guy who specialized in Mustang parts? His market fell out from beneath him because Ford stopped manufacturing Mustangs. The source dried up.

Tool

You've got to ask yourself these two vital questions:
1) Is your product line matched to your core customer?
2) Is your marketing targeted to reach your core customer?
Unless you can truly answer these with a "yes", you've got to make some changes.

It may be profitable for a while to specialize in a product no longer being manufactured. You may actually enjoy quite a markup on your ability to obtain a limited supply. But sooner or later the well will run dry. As you anticipate that drop, plan for a new core product. Remember, it takes awhile to build a reputation. Allow enough time.

Stay Focused

Many years ago in the auto salvage industry, there were the guys who handled import cars and the other guys who handled domestic cars.

This is not a joke. If you handled import cars as an auto recycler in the mid-eighties, you were considered "different" and few in the industry wanted to talk to you. By the nineties, however, that notion disappeared and it's obviously not the case today.

As the times changed, profit margins declined in domestic parts. More recyclers came into the business. Margins dropped.

That information sets the stage for a scenario from Ron's experience.

"My neighbor sees that I'm in the auto wrecking business. He owns a pizza shop. He sees that I'm driving a brand new Mercedes. He's driving a Chevy. First thing I know, he's driving a new BMW.

"He knows I'm driving a brand new Mercedes,; so he decides to open up a recycling yard. I see that he's driving a brand new BMW; so I decide to open a pizza shop.

"Before you know it, we're both broke.

"Why?

"We both stepped out of what we knew first, out of what we did well and drifted away from our core product."

The moral of the story is not to let your competition drive your future. Not all your competitors are in the same business as you. Sometimes that competitor is your neighbor, or a high school classmate, or somebody else.

If you really want to compete, stay with what you know and do best. Let your competitor change if he can't stand it. But you should stay focused on what you are doing and get better at it. He'll never be able to touch you, let alone keep up with you. The grass is often greenest on the inside of the fence.

Action!

Study your product and service lines to determine whether there are some you could eliminate without losing too much business.

Look Like Money

It is the subliminal side of selling. To be successful, you have to look successful. The auto recycling business grew out of the era where a wrecking yard was a junkyard. But neither Ron nor DL would or could have sold a junkyard to a buyer like Ford Motor Company. They wanted much more.

No matter what your business or industry is, the principles are the same. People judge you by what they see. If you're disorganized, have clutter all around your desk area, visible to your patrons, and allow pop cans, coffee cups and dust to litter the floor within eyesight of your incoming customers, do you think they will take your business seriously?

If you don't look successful, you're probably going to have a hard time being successful.

In the auto recycling industry, some operators haven't kept pace with changes in the industry. We hope some of those proprietors will read this and wake up. In all industries, the bad make it harder for the good.

Tool

In regard to how your business might look to others, prepare an objective checklist and have your mystery shopper evaluate you along with three of your competitors on these points. It may open your eyes! It will certainly help you see how you are coming across to your customers in comparison to others.

Most women would never go into some of the wrecking yards in America to buy a part because of the "junkyard" image. Likewise, most women wouldn't take a child into one. Further, if a woman was at one of these businesses with her husband or boyfriend and needed to use the restroom, she'd probably wait and go somewhere else.

People make those kinds of choices. Do you want them to do that with your business? Why send away any potential customer?

Though many operators of auto recycling yards today keep clean, well-organized locations, those who don't contribute to the negative side of the image.

It's not just true for recycling yards. Consider our example of florists. Would you rather buy flowers from an attractive, nicely organized, decorated garden shop or a trashed-up, messy, ratty-looking storefront? If the difference between places of business choice is even moderate, the nicer place will always get the most customers.

If you want to attract dollars, stand back and take a hard look at how others see you. This is a basic principle. It may be very hard to change long-entrenched habits. You may not feel you have the necessary skills to make such a change, but that doesn't matter. Hire someone to organize your yard, storefront or office. Hire someone to decorate your premises. A weekly janitorial service can make all the difference in the world as to how your customers see your operation, and it may only take an increase of one or two customers to pay for that service.

Action!

Set a goal to "fix up" at least 2 items or areas of your business next month.

Customers know it doesn't cost that much more to run a clean, well-presented business. Don't try to justify a dirty place as a way of saving money through the minimization of expenses. When you look like money, you'll attract money. Like it or not, it's human nature.

Remember, the appearance of a business is a direct manifestation of the owner's attitude toward life. Whom do you want to attract?

Management for significant gain always starts with what it has on hand. You don't have to go out and buy anything to improve the appearance of your business. Start with cleaning up, washing the windows. Start with what you have and improve on it daily. Put out the message that you are successful, that you are in business to stay in business. You want people to read "positive" and to talk "positive" behind your back.

Even a conservative operation should be kept clean and organized. It's just good for business.

If you offer warranties, the appearance of your operation can either add or take away from the confidence in those warranties, because appearance affects credibility.

Human nature is such that people talk about or at least consider what they see and experience. Ask yourself whether they are speaking or thinking positively or negatively about what they saw or experienced while at your business. Do what you can to ensure that the majority of the people go away with a pleasant remembrance of your business as well as being happy with your service.

Everyone draws a conclusion of some sort. Help your customers conclude that they stopped at a good place, not a bad one.

A positive image sets the stage for a positive sales response. Keep a well-kept, well-groomed facility, and you will attract more customers than the guy who owns the dump down the

Tool

The outward appearance of your business either adds to or takes away from the feeling of confidence in you and your products or servcies felt by your customers.

Action!

When was the last time you cleaned both the inside and outside of your windows? Do it today!

road. You will also find your customers have greater confidence in your products and that confidence will build customer loyalty. Their loyalty will in turn spread confidence to others who will become customers as well.

You might think about what your banker wants to see too. Think about the facility in which he works. He will lend money more readily to a well-groomed business. Fancy is not necessarily important to him, but he will take notice of pride, cleanliness and organizational skills. He will always respect a conservative operator who demonstrates characteristics of neatness and organization. Observing these in your operation, he will be more able to believe in your presentation. Employees also take a sense of pride from their surroundings. Attention to appearances will not only help with customers and bankers, but it will ultimately help you win community influence while establishing loyalty. With these, you achieve the ultimate gain toward significant success.

Keep up the paint, weed the parking lot, wash the windows, and sweep the floors clean every day. Change your sales signs frequently. Prepare for customers and they will come.

Likewise, if your staff members are happy, dress nicely, and greet your customers warmly, those customers will return time after time and spread the word for you. You'll have an unseen network of advertisers out there working for

Tool

A sharp looking, well-kept operation adds a strong sense of pride to your employees and, more often than not, increases the level of their work performance.

Tool

Are you turning customers away or attracting them to your business by how you keep your premises?

you round the clock.

Do you have to be rich in order to achieve this? No-not at all! You could be on the verge of dire straights. It doesn't matter how much cash flow you have in the beginning. If you, your people and your place of business all project an image of success, you'll not only survive, but, in due time, you will grow out of the tight time.

Your business may not be totally dependent on image, but it's a serious function of success. All these things work together if significance is your goal.

Appearance Matters

Did you know that personal hygiene is an indication of how you view your work? It is.

Let's suppose you are stranded on the highway. A man drives up in a beat-up, barely running, popped-up old Chevy pickup with a broken windshield. The truck has wheels of different colors. He's got a scraggly beard and hair down to his shoulders. His clothes are tattered and dirty. He leans over to role down the passenger window.

Just then, another car pulls over from the traffic lane. It's a modest 1985 Buicke in nicely kept condition. The driver is a well-groomed fellow with a smile on his face. His clothes aren't necessarily stylish, but they are clean.

Simultaneously, as if competing for your company, they chime, "Need a lift?"

With whom would you go?

Appearance makes for judgment; doesn't it? Nearly everyone would take the second offer immediately.

So this should make our point. If appearance makes a difference with strangers on the road, why wouldn't it be true for you, your employees and your place of business?

You want to look seriously at whether you or your employees are turning new customers away or attracting them to your business.

Appearance makes a difference whether it's how you and your employees look or how the business itself appears to your customers.

Polish To Shine

Many business owners reason they have made a significant improvement in their business if they just clean and paint the restrooms. But that's just not enough.

Go out and look at your delivery truck after it's loaded with merchandise, before your driver makes another delivery. Typically, in the auto parts industry, we would see a few random parts strewn around the floor, some paperwork on the dash, things hanging from the mirror, and notes stuck behind the visor. We don't even want to tell you what we could find behind the seats! There may be a little bit of oil or some such fluid on the bed of a pickup. Think about it. You have parts on these trucks, parts for sale, and parts that go for as much as five or six hundred dollars apiece! Yet many of these trucks do not have lift gates; so you can't offer full service.

Go look at one of Sears' delivery trucks. This reputable company delivers washers and dryers that cost no more than our products. In most cases you'll find a clean, well-kept truck, fully rigged. Why do we think we can deliver $500 products in run-down, beat-up trucks and expect the customers to appreciate our service? It's beyond us! It's hard to understand. It's a general misconception that runs through our industry, maybe left over from the fact that we salvage parts from wrecked cars. It's a dirty job, right?

Another important insight worth mentioning here is that many operators in the auto recycling industry keep clean trucks, use modern equipment and offer full service. But it's not uncommon in our industry for many operators who lack the necessary equipment to ask their customers on occasion to help unload a bulky or heavy part. They should never do that. Would Sears ask a customer to help unload a dishwasher? No, they wouldn't.

Why should we keep a clean delivery truck?

The reasons are simple. Today's customer is smarter than he's ever been. He has more choices as to where he'll do business. He has more advertising being thrown his way than at any other point in history. Merchants everywhere are vying for his business. He has more alternatives for choice than he's ever had in all of history. Our truck may be the point of sale for many. They may deal by phone and may never see our clean, well-organized, nicely painted, and swept place of business.

It takes more than cleaning and painting the restrooms to gain the approval and loyalty of the customers.

Making significant improvements to your business means you examine every aspect and work on polishing every aspect until your business shines above that of all your competitors.

Tool

Most of your competitors will likely never read this book let alone apply the principles we've given within its pages. What an opportunity you have in your hand with which to compete against them!

Empower Your People

Do your customers really care whether or not your operation is efficient? Maybe they do; maybe they don't. They really care more about the product they've bought from you, whether it's a good product or not, or perhaps its price. They also care a great deal about how they were serviced.

Whether your customer walks in the door or calls on the phone asking for delivery makes little difference.

Let's look at the wholesale side of our business. Say your delivery truck is out. You've got a nice truck. It's clean and kept clean. Does your driver have a radio or cell phone so you can direct him to pick up a part elsewhere? Have you empowered your driver to issue credit memos on the spot? Can he call in on behalf of a customer to see if you have other parts available for him to pick up and deliver? Does your driver give out promotional materials you've provided about your company at every stop he makes? Do you maintain an active computer database from which your staff can do an instant parts search for a customer who's ready to buy?

Our question is really whether or not your employee has the authority and equipment to service your customer right on the spot and get it done, regardless of your industry.

One of the real keys to significant success is running an operation that can take care of your customers' requests as they come to you. People like that. People like getting what they want without a whole lot of effort. Improve on ways to meet that need and you will grow in front of your competitors.

We're talking about your whole business culture in this chapter. What we've learned is

Tool

You must empower your staff to help customers. If you haven't given them that power, it's your fault when your service rating comes in as "poor quality."

Action!

Make sure your delivery driver has promotional material to hand out at every stop.

so important it should not be ignored. Image is a thing to be polished. But before you polish it, you must examine it. You've got to look in the mirror first before you can see that you need to shave this or that. You have to open your eyes when you come to work in the morning and see your business as your customers see it. You have to look around on the floor of your car and in the back seat and change what is not presentable, change it to look the way success should look. You are only dealing with habit.

Ron has a friend who, when conducting interviews with job applicants, actually goes outside to the person's car to see if there's trash on the floor and whether the car is generally unkept. If there is, the person doesn't get the job.

Once you learn that you can effect a more positive image, that it is just a matter of seeing and changing the way you do things, you will have made dramatic steps toward significant success.

Once you've lifted yourself into those new shoes, you'll see that expecting this kind of improvement from your staff is much easier. They'll respect you for it. Then you empower them. Make it possible for them to shine, too, in front of your customer.

The shine comes from continually working on buffing things up to look better and run better. As you do this, you will see that not only is your customer base increasing, but your employees are happier too. Now they can brag about their workplace. You've empowered them with tools they need to provide great service, and together you all shine. That's the picture of a company that will grow.

How This Affects The Customer

Tool

Remember, while you work on improving the quality of your business and its overall appearance, the needs of your customers are still number one!

Don't ignore your customer while you polish the frame of your business. Your customer is first. Every one of them is as important as the last one and the next one. Give them all the best attention and the best service you can WHILE you improve your business image and your approach.

If you botch the fundamentals, will you ever get your customer back for another chance? Not likely. And every customer soured is a customer putting out negative advertising.

If you don't deliver on time or provide a fair market price, you are not going to get the business. It won't matter what you're doing about company image.

We hope you understand. Nothing we're saying in these pages acts independently from anything else. Significant success happens when you rise above all your competition in all areas of your business.

Chapter 6

Perceptions

What does your customer think about you, about your business? Let's look more deeply at market perception, what it is and how important it can be to you and your business.

How do your vendors perceive you? Are they happy with you? Do they consider you fair?

How about your employees? Do they like working for you? Do they defend you? Do they brag about their work with you?

These are three important aspects of how outside perception affects your business. Fall down in one of these areas and you are far less apt to reach any degree of significant success. Excel in all three and you are well on your way.

How do you excel in the eyes of others? First, it's a matter of understanding what they see and why they see what they see. When you can put yourself in their shoes and look back at yourself and your operation honestly and objectively, you are in position to make positive, effective changes, changes that will benefit you greatly in the long run.

Consider the enormous success that both Ron and DL have enjoyed from the sale of their respective businesses in an industry not known for significant success. Why do you suppose they were approached about selling their businesses in the first place?

The corporation that bought their businesses was looking for something. The buyer's executives obviously saw something of true value in each of these businesses. What was it they saw? Why did these two businesses stand out?

We can assume the larger company approached, negotiated and purchased these two lesser companies because they saw them as leaders and niche holders in a marketplace in which they wanted to be. That assumption is fair.

As leaders in the industry, they demonstrated a spirit of pioneering by setting new standards. Even in our supporting quotes they are referred to and recognized as "pioneers". So that's one characteristic. What do pioneers do? They set the pace for others to follow. They also innovate new and better ways to accomplish things.

As leaders, these two men, Sturgeon and Fitzpatrick, have also gained considerable respect among their peers. That's influence, another characteristic of significant success.

Tool

Remember, creating a positive image sets you up for a positive future. And there's no one out there who can contribute to your positive image more than you.

What other characteristic could they have shown in order to gain significant success? It may not be as apparent, but both men feel it is the perception of "honest dealing." All those doing business with them recognize them as fair in their dealings. Perceptions are built, at least in part, by a history of actions.

Recognition

The business culture you create affects the perceptions of your customers, vendors, employees and peers.

If you're not good at creating a favorable business culture, surround yourself with people who are.

We want to have recognition for those things we achieve. That's certainly true for owners. It's probably partly why they are owners and not employees. But loyal employees want and need recognition as much as they want and need money.

As owners, we want recognition for our risk of doing business in the form of whatever rewards us and that's usually money. We want to see profits. Otherwise, we feel as though we're spinning our wheels.

Depending on the key motivation in an employee's heart, recognition can be achieved by pats on the back or through monetary rewards. The kind of recognition should fit the personality of the employee to whatever degree possible.

Fitz rewarded accomplishments through a formal annual dress banquet where they handed out plaques for top salesperson and gave safety awards for three years without an accident or injury. They also gave out attendance awards among other things that recognized the value of their employees in the eyes of the owners and their peers. That kind of appreciative recognition proved very worthwhile to the employees and the owners as well.

DL and Ron are very different personality types. This difference exemplifies the fact that there's no simple formula for success. Ron will openly admit that he wishes he had DL's "warm and fuzzy management style." DL, on the other hand, readily admits he wishes he had Ron's marketing abilities, maybe even some of Ron's aggressiveness. The point is to go with what you are, play with what you have, and don't be frustrated if you don't have all the skills required.

Recognition is also a key to customer loyalty. How do you feel when you are a customer? Do you appreciate getting the service you want, when you want it? Do you find yourself irritated when you stand around and no one seems to care that you're there for a reason? Your answer should determine your action.

Tool

Openly recognizing the positive attributes, accomplishments and skills in your staff creates a loyalty that will only serve you well. Seeing these things in your peers and others will only make you grow into being better than you are now.

Our suggestion is that you don't overlook the value of recognition because it plays a part in the motivation of not only your employees but also your customers. Give your employees the recognition they deserve. Give it to them at banquets, picnics, or luncheons. Give them recognition in the form of plaques, certificates, letters of approval, recognition in company newsletters and through bonuses. Give your employees recognition in the local newspaper when they achieve something worthy of public recognition.

For the sake of your valuable customers, teach your employees how to acknowledge customers who are standing in line. Teach them the value of looking directly into the eyes of a customer while addressing him. Your customers will advertise for you if you recognize and service their needs. There's nothing like a satisfied customer, and we're saying that a satisfied customer is a customer who goes away feeling his individual problem was both recognized and handled efficiently-even if it was just buying a product.

Recognition is uplifting. It builds morale and loyalty. It can't be false. It has to be genuine. It goes in two directions: internally and externally, from you to those who work for you and from you to those who buy from you.

Tool

Recognition is nothing more than the courteous acknowledgement of the attributes you see in others. And, nothing less! Strive to recognize the good in others and it will come back to serve you well.

Pay For Performance

Basically you want to pay your employees for the quality and results of their performance. Any employee position you can pay based on performance will enhance your bottom line. Making this transition can sometimes cause a little friction, but most employees soon learn they can actually make more when this pay relationship is established; and so they do!

Ron shifted many years ago from salary-based sales to commission-based sales. When he did, his sales figures went up by 90% in just 3 months. After that he started paying his vehicle dismantlers by the vehicle processed, rather than by the hour. Production doubled in 2 weeks.

Next he tried this with his delivery drivers, paying them by the delivery. They complained that rushing through deliveries put them at greater risk of accidents and that they couldn't be courteous to their customers or do a good job while hurrying. He asked them to look at the benchmark they'd established: UPS. They agreed that UPS drivers, though always rushed, were known to be courteous. Within weeks Ron's drivers were making 40% more deliveries each day--and they were doing this in less time!

Prior to the initiation of this plan, his drivers always came back at closing time, regardless of the number of stops they'd made. Under the

Tool

Paying commissions based on performance enhances the output of your employees because it adds an incentive to which they can directly relate.

Tool

Twenty percent of your workforce will give you 100% of their effort no matter how you compensate them; but the other 80% will positively do more work for you if they are paid based on their output.

pay per stop plan, where they had the incentive to make more stops in less time, his drivers returned early and went home early. They were happier and so were their customers.

Ron had considered adding another truck to his fleet, but following this increased performance, he decided not to do so. The result of increased driver performance caused Ron's sales to increase by about 20% at a lower cost while still using his existing fleet.

Negativity

Sometimes, no matter what you do or say, you will face an unhappy customer, vendor or employee. Maybe it will be a peer who's envious or angry for one reason or another. Some of these things are just outside your control.

Sometimes it just behooves you to separate from the person altogether. That might mean terminating your employee, no longer doing business with a particular customer or looking for a new supplier. In the case of a peer, you may just have to stay away from the person.

Let's look at each scenario separately. Joe has an employee who with fair consistency complains and gripes about the conditions the company provides. Furthermore, he is seen to bad-mouth Joe's company to customers who know nothing about the situation. Joe

Tool

Negativity in management erodes motivation and destroys attitude. If you can't correct it, you must remove it.

approaches the employee more than once, honestly tries to understand the problem and rectify it, but the negative employee continues to be negative in nearly every circumstance and in front of customers. The best thing to do is terminate this kind of person, as he is not doing Joe's business any good at all.

Tool

Don't dwell on negativity. Don't harbor it; don't patronize it; and don't perpetuate it. Negativity in the workplace takes directly away from your chances of reaching significant success.

On the other side of the counter, Joe has a particular customer who is always complaining about the work he receives or the products he buys from Joe. He's never satisfied, no matter how Joe tries to rectify the situation. Should Joe continue to try to please this customer? No. After a substantial amount of effort, Joe's best decision is to deny the customer service or product and suggest maybe he'd be happier going elsewhere.

We turn around now and see that Joe has a vendor who, unlike other suppliers, continually sends him the wrong parts. This vendor is nearly ridiculous in his dealings with Joe. He treats Joe's employees like dirt and always throws the blame back at Joe. Should Joe just buckle under and continue to use this vendor? No. Again, that kind of negativity contributes nothing to a progressive, exciting, growing company.

Don't dwell on negativity. Don't house it. Don't patronize it, and don't perpetuate it! Negativity erodes your thinking and your image. When you confront it, when it steps up in front of you, try to resolve it in a diplomatic way. Inconsistent negativity can be tolerable and even anticipated. Everybody has a bad day now and then. But when you see it consistently coming from any one source, that's your cue to dissolve the relationship and move on to better things.

If the conflict that creates negativity seems to be related to a personality clash, consider putting someone else between you and the point of conflict before terminating it. You might salvage a good worker by putting him under a different manager. You might salvage a good customer, though they may appear negative, by assigning him or her to another salesperson on your team. You might salvage your vendor relationship by staying out of the way, allowing another in your office to handle that relationship.

In some incidences perhaps an association mediator (such as the association director or president) is best suited to mitigate the circumstance.

You see? There are many ways to resolve difficult circumstances. First you try resolution. If the negativity persists unreasonably, it may be time for termination. Get out of such conflicts. Don't let them prolong themselves. They will only damage your motivation or your image.

Clearly Defined Structure

Both our companies had the reputation of being structured and disciplined. We set guidelines and stood by them. We set goals and strove to reach them.

In both cases, we've had employees tell us that they were intimidated at first when they considered coming to work for us, because they were unsure about the "rules" thing.

Auto dismantlers don't like working from a list of how they should go about taking apart a car. Salesmen don't like to be told how to make a sale.

We've learned over time that, although our employees at first don't like structure, they soon learn to appreciate it. Most of these employees who were apprehensive about working for us at first had an unstructured job at which they worked before they came to us. For example, they might be dismantling a car only to have the boss or manager take them off that job to put them on another job. When their jobs are not clearly demarked and responsibilities are not clearly defined, your employees cannot know exactly what they are expected to do or will be doing. The lack of clearly defined job tasks can create anxiety for some employees and, in turn, may cause them to function poorly.

Those who have come to us from that kind of past have taught us that a total lack of

Tool

Providing structure in your operation helps your employees understand what's expected of them and that always improves work performance!

structure simply erodes the motivation behind work. Some say that they could never second-guess what their boss was going to give them next. They had a hard time feeling good about their work. When they came to us, as soon as they got over their apprehension about any structure we might impose, they found themselves completing more and feeling good about it at the end of the day.

We don't tell them every detail. We just clearly define our expectations and make sure they understand their responsibilities. Then we let them go to work. We reward them with recognition and pay for performance when they show outstanding achievement in their results.

If you are not already doing this, you'll find that employees like structure. They like knowing exactly what you expect from them on a given day. They like achieving it. They like knowing exactly how much they're going to be paid, especially when they know that pay is based on their performance.

It all adds up to not only happier employees but also happier customers because the happiness rubs off on your customers. Given a little structure and allowed the freedom to perform individually within that structure creates maximum output.

Create a business culture where roles are clearly defined and expectations are laid-out in plain view along with attainable goals and you

Tool

You must clearly define the job duties of your employees if you expect them to perform well for you. Even in a business as small as three or four employees, duties should be clearly defined.

establish a happy employee relationship. They'll work hard for you, and they'll reflect their contentment and belief in you to your customer base.

A Strong Work Ethic

How many of you have a competitor who takes off every day? He's earned the privilege. Right? Maybe. But what does that do for his employee relations?

Tool

How's your work ethic? Now is as good a time as any to resolve to improve on it. Focus on things you can do to directly improve your business and increase your sales.

We believe that productive employees expect the owner to have a strong work ethic. Significant success doesn't come from escape, procrastination or total delegation. Going off to play doesn't do your company any good, especially if you're gone all the time. In fact, it can erode employee motivation. Employees working without a leader easily fall into poor habits and lax attitudes. It's an exceptional employee who works to excel when there's no leadership around to appreciate his or her effort. That kind of employee generally goes into business for himself. They're leaders, not followers. Followers follow leaders and, if the leaders are gone, what do the followers do?

You set the pace. You are the example. When our employees come to work, our cars are already in the parking lot. Our cars are in the parking lot when our employees go home (most days). We set the pace. We are the example.

Employees respect a boss who works hard. Lead by example.

Vendors Are Your Friends

Vendors like doing business with someone who pays them on time. That should be obvious. Pay your vendors on time. Make no excuses. If you can't pay them on time, call and tell them you can't, explain why and tell them when you can. Then hold true to your word. Vendors are not bankers. They can get very concerned when you extend your credit with them without asking.

A customer shouldn't be upset with you because he owes you money and you want it. Part of your job is to keep up on collections. When you do, 99% of the work has been done. You must get paid to survive.

Try to remember one of Ron's favorite rules for dealing with people who owe him money-"You don't have the right to be mad because you owe me money and I want it!"

Vendors also prefer doing business with those who treat their employees nicely. They will respect and favor you if you treat their employees well. Strong vendor relationships are as important to your business as strong customer relationships.

Sooner or later, your vendor will step in to rescue you from a difficult customer situation, if you have a strong relationship. Treat your vendors like they aren't important and they'll treat you the same when you need them the most. They are really your friends in the business world. Treat them like friends. Take them or their people to lunch once in awhile. Let them know you appreciate your relationship. Try to build loyalty. It works to your mutual advantage.

Employee Satisfaction

Clearly defined structure does no good, however, if you never follow up to ensure that those expectations are met.

Always be fair. If your employees are going to have bonus plans, give them the bonus plans and inform them clearly how they are going to be measured. Do this as agreed, whether you do it monthly, quarterly or yearly.

Being prompt with incentives is important. Many good employees have moved on to other opportunities because their management seemed unable to make decisions on incentives.

You don't want to beat them out of incentives exacting too much in measurements. Don't design something you know they can't make so you won't have to pay the bonuses.

That kind of dishonesty only serves to erode morale. You'll achieve the opposite of what you want to achieve.

Be fair in your dealings with your employees. Their loyalty toward you is important because, again, it ultimately flows over to your customer base. So treat your employees accordingly. If you are going to offer a bonus plan, give them one they can reach with a certain amount of honest effort on their part.

You might define an incentive like this: "If you deliver these stats by the end of this period, we're willing to pay you a bonus of such and such an amount on this date." Clearly and objectively defined, it becomes a motivator that's reachable. That's the kind of structure that will get you the results you desire most.

Achieving significant success in business requires that you build loyalty among your employees. You build loyalty in part by being fair and in part by setting goals that are reachable and bring reward when achieved.

What about your vendors? When your employees talk to one of your vendors, they are engaged, at the point of contact, in that particular vendor relationship.

To improve the quality of relationships at the point of contact, we establish an employee index that looks at the employee's level of satisfaction.

You can do this by mailing bi-annual

surveys to your employees wherein you ask the questions geared toward understanding their level of satisfaction in their work. Try to design a method that objectively scores the survey so that you can measure improvement. If it's too subjective you set yourself up for distrust or favoritism. You might also consider doing this through open round-table meetings with your employees.

Action!

Prepare and administer an employee satisfaction survey.

Ask questions like the following:

Are you allowed to do your job?
Are you happy working here?
Are the goals we set realistic?
Would you like more challenge?

The list of questions can go on and on. You can learn a great deal about your company by doing this. You will also have a better relationship with your employees because they'll feel they're being heard-that is if you respond to their answers in a favorable light. There's another benefit here, too, that should not be overlooked. You will discover ways to ensure that your employees are happier. When they are, they'll spread their happiness to both your vendors and your customers at the point of contact! More people will believe in you than ever before. You'll achieve more.

No one is the perfect leader. You can't please everyone who works for you all the time. We're not suggesting that you patronize your employees. Neither can you constantly motivate those who work for you. You can't even appreciate everyone who works for you all the time! By implementing a program, however, such as the one suggested here, you can actually reach all your employees, even in a very large firm.

Tool

You may be tempted to prepare your own employee survey, but before you do, buy a copy of the best selling book, First, Break All The Rules. The authors analyzed over 80,000 employee interviews. From their results, they provide great insight into what questions in a survey really get meaningful answers. Their expansive study produced a survey you can use. Take the survey and score the results objectively. Mail it to your employees' homes and don't require their signatures. You can track improvement in the scores by repeating the survey every 6 months or so.

Create a blind employee statisfaction survey that you conduct twice a year. Blind means that the employees don't see how the others are doing. It allows you to instigate measures that will improve your employee relationships.

Give your employees a voice and you'll grow their happiness, which in turn will spread to both your customers and your vendors. But you must show your employees that you are hearing their answers to your questions.

Internal Guarantees

Significant success is not common success; it's out of the ordinary. You are reading what we believe are the contributing factors to the success we've found. Our ideas have proven their value. Try them. See for yourself.

Business culture is something you develop. It relates directly to how others perceive you. It takes very little or no money at all to build a relationship with your customers as well as your employees. You do that by opening the door to them, seeing who they really are, listening to their real needs and following up.

Your main objective is to create an atmosphere of internal guarantees. How can you guarantee your customers that you will deliver to them tomorrow if your production staff does not guarantee the sales staff they will do whatever it takes to pull the order together on time? That's an internal guarantee.

Your objective is to give all your employees a sense of pride in their work. You are essentially asking them to "take ownership" in their responsibilities and in their department's performance.

Involve Your Customers

You want positive sales signs or signals in your customer area. You want the customer to feel he's going to get fair treatment every time he comes in. As a manager, you should be asking yourself how to serve your customer

Action!

Review your employees' responsibilities, analyzing for how they relate to your company's promises to customers.

better the next time he stops. That's giving him recognition. You are giving your customer a place in shaping your service to him.

Put a customer satisfaction index in the form of a postcard with every invoice. Design a method by which you can objectively score the results. That's how you measure improvements- and don't forget to distribute the results to all your employees.

Tool

Create a customer statisfaction index on a return postcard that you can include in the envelopes of your billing statements. Some of your customers will respond; others will appreciate your effort to discover how they are perceiving your operation.

You see these postcards in some restaurants. Most customers will not take time to fill out these satisfaction indexes and send them back. In fact, the ones you do get back will probably be the ones that complain. It's not only the answers you get back from these customers that matter, but also your image of caring left with the 95% who didn't respond to your index query. You've given them a sense of goodwill. You've said to them that you value their opinion. Most of those who don't respond will appreciate that. They'll reason that, if they had had a complaint, you were willing to listen. Further, you should answer every card that's returned. That's important.

If you do this, chances are good you'll be seen as a "pioneer" in your own industry because few small businesses, other than restaurants, conduct this kind of survey.

Perception is reality. Make your customers aware that you are interested when they have a problem. Show them they have a venue for voicing that concern. That's recognizing customers.

Strengthen Peer Relationships

Action!

Join the national, state or local association for your industry.

Your peer relationships are not unlike your vendor relationships. Your peers are the people of your own industry. They are also your associates in other businesses. You may or may not get product supplies from them, but you can always gain knowledge. When peer relations are good, you sometimes even gain business in the form of referrals, where different operators specialize in different services or products.

Your peers are going to want to know that you are honest and straightforward about your business dealings. They'll also want to know that you follow through with what you say you'll do.

Tool

It should be a business priority to attend your industry's conventions, especially those involving a tradeshow.

Show them that you care about your industry. Don't hide your findings and discoveries from them. Share them. Peer relationships can open up doorways you'd never find otherwise. The reason tradeshows around the globe have such a draw is partly due to the fact that positive peer relationships benefit those who attend them. Great insights are gained at association retreats or through rubbing elbows at trade shows.

DL and Ron met through their industry association, the Automotive Recyclers Association (ARA). Talking to each other on a regular basis brought them to the realization that they had a lot in common, and it helped make them aware they ought to share some of their ideas in print with other peers who might be missing some valuable help.

Strong peer relationships are not built by pushing everyone else around or puffing yourself up or lying. They are built by demonstrating your integrity, by representing the industry well, by offering real solutions to real problems. They're built by contributions you make to your peers through your trade association. You only gain when you give in this manner. There's no loss.

You'll go much further by working with others of like-mind. Your peers have the same problems you have. They have much the same kind of customer, certainly the same products and services. Their advice, their experience, their wisdom can be invaluable to you. Often you may not learn from your peers what to do to improve your business, but you can learn what *not* to do.

Do you think they will share it with you if you are disreputable, unreliable, dishonest and unfair? Not likely.

Tool

If you don't learn from your peers what you should do to improve your business, you will certainly learn what not to do!

Practice Integrity

Let's say you have a pond in your backyard. It's a nice pond, pretty to look at, and it has some fish in it too. When you cheat on your taxes, you put an alligator in your pond. When you cheat on your spouse, you put an alligator in the pond. When you lie to an associate, you put an alligator in the pond. Everyone puts an alligator in his own personal pond once in awhile because no one is perfect. Whether the alligators are big or small makes little difference. How many alligators, makes all the difference. Too many alligators makes the pond a dangerous place. No one will want to get near it. It will lose its prettiness. Eventually, when the alligators get big enough, one of them will jump out, grab you and pull you in.

Wouldn't it be great if your pond were really clear? Conduct yourself well. Live by moral principles, be honest in your dealings, be fair in your judgments, and pay your taxes. You may not be able to keep all the alligators out of your backyard pond, but you can control the number and size of them.

Four Simple Steps

Ron believes trouble comes in bunches. There's no such thing as luck, good or bad. We all have storms in our life. Some weather the storms better than others. By working hard and being honest, you'll find that when a storm comes your way, you will always have the money, friends and resources to see you through.

Those things you set into habit are the things that guide you when the trouble comes. If you're standing on firm ground through practiced moral principles and are developing sound business relationships, you'll weather just about any storm that comes your way.

Hopefully, by the time you've read this book, you will be ready to work on improving your business. If that's true, you will have passed a monumental milestone in your business life.

Ron says there are 4 simple steps in growing, improving or rebuilding a business. Most of your competitors, he believes, just won't get it. The first step, he says, is to recognize you have a problem. You have to see that there's room for improvement. That's where most have their downfall. Once you recognize the problem, the second step is to more closely define it. Once you've done that, then you devise a plan to address the issues you've defined. But the fourth and most difficult step is still in front of you: executing your plan. This part can be immeasurably painful because it requires a massive amount of new discipline. You'll have to deal with a whole new sector of problems because you're going to go beyond where you once were.

Chapter 7

It's All Up To You

Do you look for excuses to work less? Do you ever complain about how much money you're making?

Joe is a small business owner. He complains that he has to make more because his checks are not large enough to pay his bills. Yet whenever the mood strikes, he leaves work and goes off to do something unrelated. He escapes because he's unhappy, frustrated or stressed. His work ethic is undeveloped. He has a hard time realizing that the amount of his take-home is directly related to the quality of his work.

Joe creates the need to have big checks but fails to comprehend that, if his checks were smaller in the beginning, his business would do better. If he sacrificed in the beginning, his business would be in a much better position to provide a prosperity that would surpass his current needs.

Joe is unfocused. He has not clearly defined

his vision for the company he created. He does not take the time that's necessary to examine the details of his operation. He fails to recognize habits that hold him back and never develops the ones that would take him forward. He doesn't read a lot, seldom asks anyone else's advice and wonders why his sales are not supporting him. He's a poor manager and a lousy leader. He keeps substandard employees and keeps them in positions for which they're not suited. He can no more afford to hire the help he needs than he can to pay himself the amount he thinks he needs to take home.

Joe is a typical business entrepreneur in the start-up stages. He hasn't figured out yet that even moderate success takes not only sacrifice but also a critical self-analysis. Will Joe ever get far enough in business to decide that he wants significant success?

Maybe, but it is not likely. But he has some miles to go as far as we're concerned. Before Joe can ever hope for the kind of return he thought he'd make when he went into business, he's going to have to reorganize and recreate himself.

Across town, another business entrepreneur, Bill, is going through much the same kind of beginning. He's just not making what he wants to make. But his approach is different. He goes to work early and stays later than anyone else in his small company. He looks at every aspect of his business. He talks to customers, tries to learn what they really want or expect. He makes changes he can afford to make. He goes to seminars. He participates in his trade association. He asks his more experienced and successful peers how they did what they did. He keeps and studies his operating metrics regularly, making changes he believes will improve his business. He reads and reads and reads. Bill also takes the time to clean his place of business himself (because he can't afford to pay someone else to do it at the time) and keeps it looking sharp as a whistle.

After awhile, Bill notices that his revenue is going up. His shop seems busier than it did a year ago. He's becoming acquainted with his customers and vendors by first name. He knows many of their likes and dislikes and does his utmost to give them the kind of service they seem to like. He's even checked out his competitors, including Joe, to see how their shops look and function; he's talked to a few of their customers, even went in as a customer himself on a few occasions just to see how they treated him. He always came back with new ideas, and he always put the new ideas into play.

Two years down the road, Joe is still wondering why his paychecks are not sufficient to pay his bills. Bill, on the other hand, is enjoying a significant increase in sales and has hired an office manager, has a happy sales team and two auto dismantlers working full-time. He has more free time, but, unlike Joe, he doesn't take it. He still gets to work before anyone else and generally leaves after everyone else has gone home. Much of his time is spent analyzing the way his business operates. He also spends more time developing relationships. He takes his banker to lunch now and then, and visits his vendors to see if there may be better ways to manage their service to him.

Joe still rides the edge of obscurity. Hardly anyone knows him; they just know of him. He never goes to the association events. He seems jealous of his competitors, never shares anything about the industry, and actually runs down his competitors to his ever dwindling list of customers. He has a hundred reasons why his business is poor: a lousy location, bad weather, lack of good employees or any of an infinite number of excuses even though every competitor has their own set of obstacles.

What's the difference between these two men? Is it circumstance? Or did they actually have something to do with their "fate"?

Bill took charge of his destiny and Joe did not. Bill took every opportunity to learn more about his business, about his customers, about his peers, vendors and industry. Joe did not. Joe always put complaint first and took every opportunity to escape. Bill developed a strong work ethic. Joe became lax and lazy, justifying his bad luck on changing times and big money competition. Yet both operators were equally skilled, faced similar opportunities and had the same access to resources and mentors.

You Position Yourself

Just about everyone in America comes across a little money at sometime or another. They might win a lottery; they might inherit a sum; they might cash in some old stock that was passed on to them. Maybe they just received a modest refund on their taxes. Perhaps they had an insurance settlement from a loss or an injury in the past. We see it all the time. What do most Americans do with a cash windfall when it comes their way?

Most spend it on something they've wanted or dreamt about for a long time. Many actually put themselves into debt by using it as a down payment toward something that locks them up with monthly payments.

Few put their windfall to work to grow it. So after a time, long or short, it's gone.

If money comes your way in any form, don't throw it away flamboyantly. Invest it in what you are doing or in something that will likely ensure its growth. Use it to position yourself. Use it to meet new business contacts. Both Ron and DL firmly believe there are only a few such opportunities that come in a person's lifetime.

Tool

You position yourself. Nobody else is responsible for your position in the marketplace. Next time you receive even a small windfall, use it wisely and try to grow it into something larger.

Some people use money opportunities wisely; some don't. Ron calls these opportunities "monetary crossroads." You should take them when you cross the junction.

Very few people recognize these life-changing opportunities. When Ron was fresh out of high school, his dad passed away and left him an old VW to drive. Ron went into business working on cars, opening a little VW repair shop. But he soon learned it was a tough way to make a living. In 1973, 2 years after he started, a check showed up in his mail for $2,000. It was the balance leftover from $4,000 his father had left for Ron's college. As Ron had stopped going to college, his father's executor sent him the remaining balance.

Ron decided he wanted to deal in cars as well, so he bought a used '71 VW Bug with the money and sold it for $2500, taking a '71 Ford Pinto in trade on the deal. He'd made more in those two transactions in one week than he did working on cars; so he decided he wanted more of that action. Within 6 months, while still working on cars for a month, he had a $10,000 financing floorplan at his bank and was regularly buying and selling cars.

That one check for $2,000 completely changed his life. He had recalibrated his financial ambitions and was moving into a new area of business life. You position yourself for success. Nobody does it for you.

Create The Passion

You should know by now whether the achievement of significant success is a true desire in your heart. Do you want it badly enough to make the necessary sacrifices? We've shown you some of what it takes. We've shown you what we think has made the difference for us.

Our next question is for your personal answer: do you have the passion? That might be a tough question. Only you know the answer, and it really only matters to you. But you've got to have passion. You have to want success enough to give something up, to forego something today. Different people have different levels of passion and show it in different ways.

Ron always says he is shot out of bed on a rocket and his hands shake for the need to be at work. (He's quick to point out, however, that different folks hold different levels of ambition and that not everybody's like him.)

The difference between Joe and Bill in our character scenario at the beginning of this chapter is that Bill didn't have to sacrifice family relations. He made the necessary sacrifices of self in order to gain a stronger position. He had a passion that Joe did not have. When the stress became great, Bill stayed put; Joe escaped. When the finances were uncertain, Bill applied himself; Joe avoided change.

Do you think there was a difference in the beginning between these two stereotypical entrepreneurs? They started about the same. Neither had a lot with which to work; both had an idea. One worked hard; the other complained a lot. One educated himself whenever he could and kept on gaining knowledge; the other became more remote, more obscure.

The primary difference between these two characters was visible in the beginning; it was the difference in their private sense of passion. Bill wanted success enough to sacrifice for it, to put off gratification of temporary fulfillment for a stronger business position. Joe just had no desire to go further than where he was in the beginning. His lack of motivation led to a place where he just didn't care. He threw the blame elsewhere, took none of it himself. He basically acted like a weak employee rather than the owner or entrepreneur he purported to be.

Do everything in your grasp to crystallize a strong vision for a highly successful career. Look at the characteristics of others who already hold a position of success. Imitate them. Emulate those characteristics. Develop the passion in your heart by sharpening the vision of where you'd like to be. Make a three-year plan. Make a five-year plan. Create a ten-year plan. Maybe it will seem very difficult for you to do this. You'll probably find that the further out you

Action!

Put your 3, 5 and 10 year plans in writing and review them periodically.

look, the more vague the vision becomes. Maybe you don't yet really know where you want to go, who you want to be.

Create the passion; then apply yourself.

The Pattern Of Habit

It becomes a way of life. Your early decision to set things aside for tomorrow's gain becomes a habit that stays with you for life. That's one of the differences between Bill and Joe in our scenario. Both started equally, but one failed in a downward spiral while the other gained at almost every point. The difference was in the pattern of habit each had created in his work ethic.

When Ron started his business he received loans from 2 friends who evidently saw his potential. One was his accountant; the other was his attorney. Each man loaned Ron $20,000 in exchange for a 2% return on sales for 6 years, with a final payment of $20,000 at the end of the term. At that time, Ron's gross sales were around $3200 a month; so the investment might have been a sure risk with a long time to return. Perhaps they recognized that Ron was energetic. Maybe they could see he had passion. Regardless, they loaned him the money. By the end of the third year, Ron was paying both men $1500 a month each on that $40,000. By the end of the fourth year, Ron had paid them each $65,000 on that 2% royalty, and they were still due $20,000 each at the end of the 6-year period. Ron went to his investors and said, "Hey, let's be fair! I went through the twenty-grand more than four years ago and you've both gotten a lot more than you ever thought you would. I'm asking you to let me pay you back your $20,000 and let me out of the debt."

Both of them did. This illustrates both passion and sacrifice. Ron wanted his business badly enough to take a high-risk loan. He was willing to sacrifice as well in order to pay it back as he had agreed. He demonstrated two more characteristics you shouldn't miss: integrity and creative problem-solving.

Both investors had made considerable money on the risk they took in Ron. He honored their returns and would have continued, without argument. But a sense of concern stepped in and caused him to exercise yet another characteristic of the truly successful: creative thinking.

Imagine the pleasure his two friends might have felt when they realized their "investment" had grown up? This is an example of what it takes to become successful. You create a passion and adhere to it through all things that confront you in business.

Chapter 8

A Greater Tomorrow

Today's sacrifice is tomorrow's gain. We've all heard that a hundred times. It's a cliché. You have to sacrifice today for a bigger tomorrow. How does it apply to your current situation?

Do you really want to do what you're doing? Do you REALLY want to do it? If you just want a job, go get a job and put this book back on the shelf.

You have to be in love with what you do. If you're doing it for any other reason than the fact that you love it and want it, it won't work. That's the foundation of a persevering attitude.

Case in point: Ron used to live in a mobile home. It was a conservative setting. He'd get up early in the morning and go to work. In the evening he'd come home to his mobile home. One day when he returned he discovered to his horror that the mobile home right next to his was on fire. It was already engulfed and out of control. As fast as he could, he hooked up his garden hose to water down the roof of his own home, which he thought he was going to lose at any moment. Just in time, firemen came and doused the burning trailer. Ron's home survived.

Relieved if not somewhat stunned, he went into his home, sat down and opened the mail. The first letter was from the IRS, a notice they were going to audit him!

Was that a bad day? Wow! He nearly lost his home; now he had to face the indomitable IRS. What would he do?

What would you do?

Ron got up the next day and went to work as he always did. He was the first one there and the last one to leave. He survived the fire and he survived the audit. Why? He'd developed the habit of a persevering attitude.

This attitude of perseverance and resilience regardless of circumstances has to become a way of life. At the root of it is a passion for what you are doing. You're not about to give up.

The older you are, statistical data show, the less likely you are to take risks. As you get older, you become inherently more conservative. It's easier for older entrepreneurs to settle into what they have. They are less apt to reach out toward a greater tomorrow.

This is a universal norm. Perhaps you are the exception. There most certainly are exceptions to this, as there are exceptions to any kind of average pattern. We present this because we want you to examine whether your

Tool

Learn to be more resilient. Don't fight battles you can't win and don't wring your hands fretting over circumstances outside your control. Save your energy and creativity for situations you can control.

sense of "today" has become a way of life. Are you just accepting what you have or do you have a hope for a greater tomorrow?

Settle for the daily grind and your passion will fade. Fall asleep in the habits of routine and your creativity will dwindle. You'll take fewer risks. Tomorrow may never be more than what you have right now.

The only way to avoid this, the only way to reach for significant success is to attack both the good and the bad habits with passion. Find and rekindle that which makes your hands shake until you can get to work. Get up, wake up, shake your head and look in the mirror! Are you satisfied with what you've achieved?

Do You Really Want It?

One way to rekindle your passion is to give yourself an examination. You can do this mentally. Ask yourself, "What do I do for escape?"

When the going gets tough, what do you do? When your mobile home nearly burns to the ground and the IRS knocks on your door, what do you do? When you have a comfortable dollar amount coming in every year, what do you do? When a bigger competitor moves into your neighborhood, what do you do? What do you do when you're broke? What do you do when the bills far outweigh your income?

When the idea of a "greater tomorrow" seems ridiculous, what do you do?

What you actually do should give you a clue. If you go out to play or avoid serious issues, perhaps you've already accepted your situation. If you look forward to retirement and say to yourself, "Oh well, I guess I've done enough," then maybe you have. If you go gambling, then you're looking in the wrong direction for a greater day.

Significant success does not come to anyone by luck. Neither is it found by retreating into a game or some other form of escape. Defining what you do for escape provides a clue to the habits you've developed as a business entrepreneur. But don't overlook the importance of balance. Family and recreation are important to a healthy state of mind and a positive business attitude. You make the choice.

If you want significant success, you'll have to work on those habits that build it. Go to work early. Get there first. Be the last to leave. Use every snippet of time you can to accomplish something. Analyze your operation in detail. Watch your competitors. Mimic them where their traits seem successful and avoid those patterns that detract from their business.

No one can do this for you, not even this book. We can't instill in you anything more than a temporary notion. If you don't have a

Tool

Work on developing habits that ensure success. Go to work earlier and leave later if that fits your ambitions. Stay in the thick of it when the going gets tough. By studying the habits of successful people, you'll find ways to improve your own.

persevering attitude and yet say you want a greater tomorrow, you'll probably fail. The persevering attitude comes from your heart; it comes out of the stress; it grows out of the difficult times. It is found in your desire. Do you REALLY want it?

Your Situation Doesn't Matter

As a fourth generation manager, DL faced a very different set of circumstances than Ron. Ron had to initiate his own incentives and find his mentors. DL had strong mentors in front of him who basically required him to initiate his own incentives.

"Going to work for Dad" wasn't enough for DL. It was a notion he fought in the beginning. Initially, the idea of working for his father and grandfather didn't mean enough to him. He wanted more. As he matured, however, he began to see that he could attain more by carrying on where they left off.

DL's motivation, the root of his passion, was found in his desire to prove himself regardless of the inside position. Once he answered the question that he was in it for his own goals, then he had to prove not only to his family and self but also to the employees that he could "earn" the privilege of enjoying a high level of success. DL found the desire. He found the motivation to excel inside his own being. Nobody put it on him. No one drilled it into him. His passion to succeed rose out of his desire to attain.

The desire to succeed in a significant way can rise from considerably different circumstances. No one comes into business from the same background. Some have advantages others don't have. Our circumstances at the start may differ considerably. What we do with those circumstances is defined by our passion.

So the question becomes, "Do I have the passion?" It's the same question for all of us. The answer is found in what you do. It's seen in the actions reflected by your habits. If your habits are allowed to develop poorly, the path is counter to progress. If your habits are allowed to develop badly, then perhaps you're turned around and walking directly away from any degree of real success.

Do you have control of your habits? Can you change them? You bet! Yes, indeed! Look at what you can change and make those changes. If you need to spend more time at work, then do that. If you need to take more time off to relax and think creatively, do that. Everyone is different. Only you can make the choice that is right for you.

When you get a little money coming in, invest it in your business, at least in the early years. Put it into more or better equipment. Don't slip off to some island retreat. Don't buy

Tool

Look at what you can do to improve yourself by listing your weaknesses on paper. Don't hold back. You don't want to lie to yourself. Once you recognize a weakness, you'll have something you can improve upon.

that new set of golf clubs. Don't settle for mediocre gain when you haven't reached your goal. Little rewards are fine; but learn to sacrifice today for a better tomorrow. This is a habit you can control. You can grow it, no matter what your circumstances may be.

When DL was still a kid, between the ages of 11 and 18, he worked part time on the weekends in his dad's shop. The jobs were simple, if not mundane: cleaning up oil spills, sweeping floors, organizing nut and bolt drawers, stacking pallets. He wasn't forced to do this. He was given the opportunity to earn money helping out in his dad's shop.

During all that time, DL was reinforced with the thought that at anytime, if he got the notion he could do better elsewhere, he was free to go.

With that freedom, DL took a janitorial job at his church working weekends and evenings in his late teens. At one point, he was working the janitorial job as well as delivering pizzas on Friday nights. He was making good money for a high school boy going to school full time.

During his first two years of college, he'd return on summer break and work at Fitz for his dad. There, he admits even today, he found frustration because he was on the bottom. He felt he could do his own thing. One day in a discussion, his father told him that he didn't need to stay in school, he was free to do whatever he chose to do. But in regards to the

Tool

Stay with your plan regardless of the challenges and obstacles that crop up in front of you. Perseverance will carry you through, but stay with your plan!

Fitz operation, he wasn't going to manage unless he had the education. He could always have a job, but management was out until he was qualified. In short, his dad insisted he have a degree or he couldn't manage.

That bothered DL considerably because of his young-man's pride. He knew there were other managers in the company who did not have a degree and couldn't understand why his father was so adamant about a degree for himself. He saw it as a hard stance to take.

So in his third collegiate summer, he came home, got his own apartment and resolved to do his own thing. He took on two jobs: one as a UPS night shifter sorting packages from 1:00 to 5:00 in the morning; the other, working for the Red Robin restaurant chain, first as a bus boy, then as a waiter.

The extra workload forced DL to slow down his studies to part-time, but he stuck with the schooling and graduated after five years.

At graduation, his father said, "Now that you have your schooling, I'd like to offer you a position. If you'd like to come in, you can enter as a buyer's trainee. You've proven you can stick with something. I think you are capable of getting into management, and we'd like to have you come on board."

In retrospect, DL is thankful that his father never forced him to accept the opportunity. He also appreciates that it wasn't handed to him on a silver platter.

"He made me realize you have to believe in yourself and you have to develop the habits of a hard work ethic and the desire for success. No one can hand them to you."

The training worked. Three years later, DL was back asking if he could go back to school in the evenings to obtain a Masters Degree. He wanted to do that on top of working sixty to seventy hours a week.

His dad agreed. A year into the graduate program, DL earned the spot of General Manager in the Fitz corporation.

DL's drive gives you a hands-on experience of what it takes to reach significant success. It is never easy, and it never happens quickly.

By DL's example we see that the wisdom of requiring higher education was passed on to him from his father. It wasn't the education that mattered as much as it was the persevering attitude and self-confidence that grew out of his "sticking with it". DL showed character in deciding on his own to go further with a Masters Degree. He completed that while serving as General Manager with a lot of duties and responsibilities in addition to having a family of his own.

A strong work ethic is born out of challenge, but it only comes to those who meet that challenge.

Tool

A strong work ethic comes to those who meet the challenges head on and don't let obstacles stop them. If you don't have a strong work ethic, you can develop one by refusing to shrink back when the going gets tough.

No Cap On Achievement

Work on your habits. Be self-critical about where you go for escape, about what you do to get out of strenuous, difficult or stressful situations. It's right in the middle of all those tough times that the steel of your character is forged. Those who stay in the thick of it, analyzing their way through, are the ones most likely to find the pathway to success.

How would you define "passion" and compare it to "persevering attitude" in the business situation?

If you are working only for money, you are doing it for the wrong reason. Money may flow and it should be the result of your work, but your motivation has to be other than money, or passion is not present. There may be some who disagree. We can't help that. We can only give you our experiential point of view. Money does not by itself bring on a passionate devotion to work. Money, in and of itself, will not provide you with the staying power you need in developing a persevering attitude.

Passion in our reference means that you want to do what you are doing because you get a certain inner satisfaction from doing it.

Earlier in this book we might have given you the impression that work is always about money. To clarify, money plays a huge part in the description of success, but success is not

Tool

Passion for your work is the root of achievement. If you don't have passion, you have to find it because it's necessary for you to go beyond where you are now.

really about money. Success is about self-satisfaction.

If it were only about money, then when the money is in short supply (as it inevitably is at one time or another on everyone's path), you lose momentum. If you get a certain satisfaction from doing what you do, you are likely to grow the persevering attitude that we're saying is essential to reaching your chosen level of success.

Some passionate entrepreneurs grow their business, gain lots of positive peer recognition, and work hard, but don't attain the significant success we are promoting because they don't add the planning, measuring and adjustments necessary. DL and Ron can't provide the passion, determination, and willingness to sacrifice; but they can offer several common sense solutions to improve your chances for significant success.

Everyone runs into roadblocks. Everyone bumps into surprises. Everyone has difficulty. Everyone in the position of ownership runs low on revenue at one time or another. It's having a persevering attitude that pulls you through.

Those who develop escape mechanisms find eventually that escape is the path they take. Those who develop persevering attitudes find eventually that their reward is where they always knew it was: on the other side of difficulty.

Tool

A persevering attitude grows out of your choice to "stay with it regardless" in hard times as well as good times and always look for ways to improve.

What gives birth to that "certain satisfaction" about which we're writing? It's the passion you foster by the choices you take on your way to the dream you have. It comes out of the desire you harbor to prove to yourself or to others that you can reach your dream. It's proof to your competitors that you are better at the game than they are. It's found in showing your parents that you can take the baton and run farther because they ran a good race and you learned from them.

A persevering attitude comes from the combination of loving what you do, holding the willingness to sacrifice and the willingness to work harder than most of your employees and all of your competitors.

One of Ron's competitors, Walter Williams, shed light on this one day when he said, "Ron, the reason you are successful is because you keep shooting the gun. Everybody else shoots the gun and then they lay it down and take off for a month or two." He was alluding to the fact that Ron just kept on working until he surpassed his competitors and then kept on working as if there were no limit.

Pay attention to that. Ron has demonstrated, like DL, that persevering attitude means there's no cap on achievement.

In our definition above, loving what you do means you have a passion for it; the willingness to sacrifice means you're willing to forego that large paycheck in order to see your business through a dry time; and the willingness to work harder than others means you're willing to stay put and keep on because your satisfaction is found in walking on the path you've selected.

Every Snippet Of Time

Ron is known in his industry for his ability to utilize even the smallest bits of time. He's been known to talk on his cell phone while using the men's room. Though that may seem funny, it actually demonstrates an important characteristic of the extremely successful-the efficient use of time.

Ron is also known for his exceptional ability to delegate. Call him a workaholic. It won't matter to him. He's in his office earlier than anyone and leaves later-not because he's worried-because he's pushing for something greater, wants something bigger.

Ron doesn't advocate being a workaholic. He advocates finding your passion. From the passion, he'll tell you, rises the staying power, the ability to forge ahead through difficulty. Ron has developed his efficient use of time because as the reality of accomplishment looms, time is too short. Can't get it all done. Got to pass it on to others. Got to delegate. His satisfaction is found in the accomplishment of much.

What are some of the ways you can add at least an hour of productivity to each day? Use a PDA to organize your notes and keep track of your objectives more efficiently. Don't play phone tag! Use a fax machine (or email) to communicate with people who are hard to reach. Use your cell phone whenever possible. Carry your callback list with you (preferably on your PDA) and make those calls while you're waiting at the doctor's office or work on something else while your computer reboots. You will be amazed how many snippets of time are available to you in any given day. Add them together and they total up to a significant amount of time.

You can also host early morning meetings with your managers, vendors or other important people. On the management side, preventative maintenance will save you time as well as money.

When you're in your car between meetings or going to and from work, you may be able to handle two or three pieces of business on your cell phone (though laws may require you to pull over in some states). Technology is now to the point where you can add voice-activated calling and speakers to your cell phone for safe driving while you talk. You'll crop that out of the twenty minutes you'd otherwise have to take

Tool

When you realize how much you can get done in little snippets of time, you'll start looking for more ways to utilize time efficiently.

Action!

Create an on-going list of ways to isolate snippets of time and write what you plan to do in them.

later in the day in your office.

If you can accomplish something other than nature's call while using the restroom, why not do so?

Utilizing time efficiently is utilizing time to further your advance on the path toward significant success. Time is your friend if you use it correctly; your enemy, if you don't.

Chapter 9

How You Get There

How many times do we see business owners looking out the window or at their watch while impatiently waiting for the time to justify their exit?

Why come in late or leave early if your ambition is to excel?

Those who are always looking for excuses not to work are never going to enjoy the fruits of success. The reason is simple. They develop the habit of excusing themselves from work. They develop the habit of escaping from work.

On the other hand, those who develop the efficient use of time are developing an ability to expand their futures. Let's fall back on the scenario between our imaginary Joe and Bill. Joe is the one who fades into obscurity. Bill is the one who finds varying degrees of success early in his career and goes on to experience significant success. One of the primary differences between the two is found in their use of time.

From the start, Joe justified reasons why he could leave early. He looked for excuses to get out of work whenever he could and eventually he found those excuses every time he looked. He had a pocket full of them. He carried them around and was ready to roll them off his lips whenever things looked difficult. He thought he was happy, but in reality he was quite unhappy. He just wasn't finding satisfaction in his work.

On the contrary, Bill seemed to accomplish everything he desired. Early on in his work life, he learned that there was always something to do: a floor to be swept, something he could study, a phone call he could make. He utilized every shred of time and never made an excuse to avoid anything in his path. He met his challenges head-on and seemed to enjoy the rough times, as though he knew it would get better.

Bill was ready to sacrifice whenever the moment called for it. Joe was always reluctant. A sacrifice to Joe was giving up a game of golf because the work demanded it. A sacrifice to Bill was taking less home because the business demanded it.

The differences between these two hypothetical characters grow more evident as time goes on. Remember, they started pretty

Tool

The creation of good work habits enhances your ability to expand on your future and greatly increases your odds of success.

much on equal ground. Neither one had much in the beginning. One attained a great deal; the other found obscurity. One enjoyed the route; the other hated it.

What's the common thread? How can we define what they were both doing so that we can emulate the successful one and rid ourselves of the characteristics of the unsuccessful one?

We do it by recognizing that it's all housed in the habits they chose to develop. Bill chose to develop habits that would lead to his success. Joe chose the contrary path. Bill found satisfaction along the way and never ran out of goals to achieve. Joe found only an increasing sense of dread and unhappiness.

"Ah, but to escape," Joe thought, while Bill looked for ways to expand his horizons and take on even more. The outcome of each man's life was really hidden in the habits they chose to develop.

Strong Habits Count

You might have gathered by now that Ron and DL differ on many counts, but both are extremely successful. Though they have different backgrounds and skills, different management styles, they both found success. Both were innovators in their industry. In these ways, they parallel characteristics of our successful fictional model, Bill.

Ron on the one hand, as described by his peers, is "intense and audacious" while DL is often described as "structured and conservative". The root of passion varies from one person to the next. What motivates one does not necessarily motivate the other. So if the degree of passion varies, it is a personal thing and must be found in one's private thoughts, in the makeup of one's own being, vision and dreams.

You don't have to be an intense workaholic to find significant success. Neither do you have to be a structured pragmatist. The common thread in character is that both Ron and DL have developed strong habits that support their work ethic and back up their decision-making. You should see this same characteristic in our fictional depiction of Bill.

We're pointing this out so you won't miss it. You can be any kind of person having any kind of personality found in the business world. It's not so much what kind of person you are as it is what you do with what you are. That's what really counts.

Have some phone calls to make today? If you have a Palm Pilot or similar device, you already have the phone numbers you need. If not, write them down on a piece of paper and take them with you, so that on the way you can make those calls, using every snippet of time. Who knows, you might have to use a bathroom somewhere along the way; but that shouldn't keep you from getting some business done, should it?

Two Kinds Of Risk

Are you willing to risk?

If you want to leverage yourself in order to reach a higher income or attain more, you'll have to take risks. If you don't want mediocrity, if you don't want to ride through life in the middle of the road, you are going to face risk every step of the way. When you stop risking, you fall into mediocrity.

You are responsible for everything that happens (or doesn't happen) to you in business. The risks you take determine the return that comes your way. But there are two kinds of risk.

One is foolish risk. It is reckless, without thought or care. The foolish risk taker throws caution away. This kind of risk can lead to demise in a hurry. Some call it "bad luck", but we don't.

The other kind is calculated risk. It incorporates thought, inspection, planning. Calculated risk considers the numbers. A good risk taker considers all aspects before the event or move takes place so that he knows ahead what he could gain and holds the possibility of

Tool

A good risktaker considers all aspects of the outcome of his action before he takes it.

an early exit before he ever starts. He's a good game player. Some call him "lucky", but we don't.

Our fictional Joe had gotten more and more into the habit of taking foolish risks in his business ventures. To him success is a gamble. "Dang," he says, "I just can't get lucky." But he believes he'll get lucky someday, "Maybe today." The poor man has been blinded by earlier choices that led to the development of poor judgment. He has no real work ethic. He escapes whenever he can, especially when the going gets rough.

Bill, on the other hand, has developed good habits. He doesn't believe in luck because he's not a gambler. He plans everything. Once in awhile he enters into a risky situation and sees that it's going bad; so he pulls out in time and loses nothing except perhaps a little pride. But even there, he reassures himself with the knowledge that he "won't do that again".

Bill learns from his mistakes.

Joe does not.

One is a foolish risk taker; the other is a calculated risk taker. There are risk takers of every degree from the absolutely foolish to the overly cautious.

Good risk taking involves doing your homework. You want to use your operating metrics to make sound decisions. You don't want to guess or speculate on the actions you

Tool

Most of us know that successful people learn from their mistakes. The secret is in not repeating the mistakes. Then you're on your way to success!

should take. Good risk takers are careful thinkers who plan ahead. But they don't stay on the drawing board. They get off the dock and go for the swim because they can see potential gain from the risk. Planning is a mental way of calculating whether something is worthwhile or not. Good risk takers weigh the odds, mark the path and hold onto an escape route. In addition, because they have analyzed the situation, they seldom make the same mistake twice.

Delegate Effectively

As owners, we tend to be possessive of our idea. After all, it was our brainchild; right? The problem is that many owners make the mistake of trying to do everything themselves. If you are going to move on to greater heights, however, you're going to have to master the subtle art of delegation. Rulers are called rulers because they rule. Managers are called managers because they manage.

Learning to delegate effectively is one of the requirements of the very successful. Someone good at delegating is someone who has learned how to hand tasks over to others for accomplishment but retain control.

How do you get there? You have to recognize and hire people who can accept

Tool

Take a good look at the tasks you currently do yourself to see what can be delegated to someone else. Your purpose is to create more time for high level planning.

authority. You have to delegate to them, let them make mistakes, correct them, guide them. You have to lead people, work with them, motivate them and rehabilitate them when they have problems. They will have problems.

You are also, as an owner, going to have to accept mediocrity in performance because most people who work for you do not have the same motivation you have. They have a job. You have a dream. They have a need for pay. You have ambition. Most of them just want to get by and be happy. You want to attain greater things and that makes you happy. So, because of these differences, most of those to whom you delegate various tasks will not perform them the same way you would if you did it yourself. You may have to tolerate varying degrees of mediocrity in performance. Otherwise, you'll go stark raving mad and no one will work for you!

This is a description of what you'll find when you reach out beyond yourself on the path to greater attainment. It's not a reflection on employees. Of course you will have employees who do not act or perform perfectly. Neither will they make decisions all the time the way you would make decisions. Their motivations are different. You will find some people are much better at certain functions than you are. For example, buying requires discipline and diligence rather than creativity. Accounting

Tool

You will always impede your growth if you try to do everything yourself. Get rid of the attitude that only you can do it right because that's not true.

requires attention to detail; marketing, a flair. You want to align the skills and talents of those you hire with functions they are inclined to do best.

Successful entrepreneurs learn to delegate and thereby learn how to motivate and lead people who have lesser goals, lesser standards and different motivations.

What To Expect

What will you do, or what do you do when your employees, some of whom may be highly qualified, stand up and say something is not going to work? You have a terrific idea. You've thought about it, considered the risk and wish to venture forward. But as you begin to delegate responsibilities you find disbelief among your troops. They don't think it can be done. What do you do?

This is a defining moment. It's a challenge that comes to everyone who attains to greater success. What do you do?

Let's consider our good man Bill. He's proven himself as a candidate for significant success because he's developed not only the good habits and the work ethic that accompanies them, but he's learned to take calculated risks as well. He enters into a new venture with due caution and knows he can

Tool

Learn to listen to your staff. They work almost every day in the same industry as you and may hold insights that will greatly improve your business. But you'll never learn anything from them if you don't listen to them.

pull out before it's too late. So he brings a good idea to his trusted staff and begins to layout the plan in front of them.

As the plan unfolds, he finds that his people are objecting on one point or another. He looks at them with surprise. Can't they see what he's saying? Can't they see that if the team accomplishes his plan, the company would be stronger in the marketplace?

Still they object. He can't detect the reasons. Something's amiss and he can't figure it out. No matter how he explains, though he knows they'll do it if pushed, he senses their lack of appreciation for the idea. What does Bill do?

His rebuttal is to question the source of complaint. "Alright. If you don't think this will work, tell me why."

Experience has taught Bill not to push people by force. He knows that if he lords it over them against their beliefs, they'll perform poorly and probably ruin the opportunity. He knows if they don't "buy in" and take ownership, they won't be enthusiastic and will not likely accept the responsibilities that will come with the new direction. His wisdom makes him reluctant to proceed without full commitment.

But at this point, he sees that no one has objected with a solid reason; so he tries to draw out any reticent feelings. "Tell me why it won't work."

If they can't explain why in clear, convincing terms, he'll give the command to proceed. If they can, perhaps they saved him from making a mistake. If they are convincing, Bill can only appreciate their candor and devotion.

You don't want to be autocratic. You want to encourage input, as Bill is doing. He has surrounded himself with people who add value. If they're stuck, he's stuck. So he's looking to find out why before proceeding with his idea. He knows the value of consensus.

However, there is one more thing to consider in this kind of internal court. Some employees can increase a risk because they don't believe your plan can be accomplished. We suspect that our hero Bill would spot such a person through day-to-day contact. If such an employee were to rise to the surface during this hypothetical discussion, Bill would discern their weakness in belief. He knows he cannot delegate to a person who truly believes it can't be done. Their lack of belief would undermine their performance and erode their creativity. He would be better off to set them on another task or let them go. He knows he can't have a sour apple in the barrel.

Our point is that every situation is different, but some risks are grave enough that having non-believers in the pack is a crippling factor. Good people are sometimes hard to come by. Bill has learned that, if he doesn't have good

Tool

Don't take the risk if too many of your employees don't believe it can be done. If you can't convince them and still want to proceed, you might consider replacing the more doubtful ones because they will only hinder your progress with negativity.

people on board, some risks aren't worth the taking.

The Best Way To Delegate

When DL first came into his management position, he was responsible for putting all the numbers together on end-of-year projections for the following year. His father sent him back to the calculator more than once because he knew DL didn't have the projections right. Rather than do the work for him, his father sent him back to rethink the numbers until he learned to think it through properly and on his own. This is another form of management technique.

You want to train your delegates by having them go through the mistakes themselves. Make them do it. It's the forging of the steel in this manner that will create the team you desire to have. You don't want just *followers*. You want *accomplishers*. Accomplishers are people who are capable of taking on a task themselves and completing it. You don't train them by doing it for them. You must require that they learn what you are delegating.

Remember, the real gain was the self-confidence DL acquired as he matured from the experience. The praise was, "Now I know you can stick with it." A virtue had developed in DL that would be necessary for the tough

Tool

Remember, you're not training people if you do their job for them. Give them some room to make mistakes, just as you have as you learned.

management decisions that would come later. Furthermore, the habit of perseverance he established was every bit as important as the lessons!

In one specific instance, to better illustrate, DL worked closely with his father while learning to forecast budgets. DL's delegated responsibility was to explain the financials to his dad. During those times there were often differences between what had been budgeted and what was actually there. DL's father would require DL to explain the difference. The father would not do it for the son.

"Well, it's close," DL would say. But his dad never accepted the term "close."

"Why is it off? I want you to tell me why it's off," his dad would counter, especially on things like real estate taxes, insurance payments, things of that nature.

In this one instance, the figures on an insurance payment were double the projected cost.

"Maybe it's just timing," DL parried.

"No, it's not timing because we thought that out in the budgeting process. Go back and analyze it until you can tell me why."

As a young manager, DL would have believed his numbers but, on re-examination, found that the company had inadvertently made a double payment. It was $10,000 too much. It was an embarrassment for the young

DL, but an incredibly valuable lesson. Had his father pointed it out to him rather than forcing him to come forth with the answer, DL might never have learned the lesson. To this day, DL practices the same technique of requiring an explanation until satisfaction is reached. His managers learn to think through things and bring valid projections forward without wasting time.

Chapter 10

Calculated Approach

How do you promote your company? There is so much noise out there in the form of advertising that you must address this issue, or you won't climb above your competitors. If people don't know you are in business, you won't have customers. This is just as true for the virtual business (on the Internet) as it is for the shop on the street.

Are marketing and advertising the same thing? Many people believe they are. The typical small business makes this assumption. They don't think about marketing because they are advertising somewhere in some small way.

A good location can compensate for a poor understanding of marketing, but that's an exception to the rule. Properly run and marketed businesses routinely excel in poor locations. Marketing is the crafted means of letting people know you are in business and where they can find you. Advertising is paid

Tool

Strive to truly understand the differences between marketing and advertising. Too many business owners only advertise; few really understand the immense value in marketing.

promotion. You might channel revenue into marketing, perhaps even contract a marketing firm-but that's not the same as advertising or contracting an advertising company.

Marketing has many, many forms. It's press releases, magazine articles, newspaper articles, and interviews. It's company participation in public events. It's participation on a private level on public boards. Marketing is contacting people who can influence others and stimulate awareness of your market presence. Effective marketing is even having your banker speak favorably of you when you are not present. Marketing is having a customer refer your business to a friend.

How are these things achieved? Do they happen because your doors are open between 8:00 a.m. and 5:00 p.m.? No. Marketing does not just happen. It is a calculated effort that comes from planning.

Understand there is a difference between marketing and advertising. Marketing your company successfully must come first and is more important than advertising your products and services. For a better understanding, ask yourself who your customer is and where your market is.

In the auto recycling industry, not everyone driving a car is a potential customer. In the floral industry, not everyone is a potential customer to buy flowers.

Tool

The knowledge of how to market yourself starts with your business plan. That's where you should see what you need to do to market your business better.

Tool

Remember, identify your customer then match your product, service and marketing to that customer.

An Example In Hand

We've gone through this same process in marketing How To Salvage Millions From Your Small Business. We first determined that our primary readers were owners in the auto-recycling industry. We know by our relationships that most of these readers have limited time to read business books. If we could get them to read this, we concluded, we'd be doing something significant already.

We figured that in order to make this book effective, we'd have to create tools they could easily apply and place them in the margins for quick reference. So we did that.

We also reasoned that our primary readers wouldn't buy enough books to justify our effort; so we slanted it toward general market small-business entrepreneurs (with less than 100 employees) who might be hungry for more success than they've had to date.

The example you're holding in your hands should serve to illustrate our point: you must understand your market.

In this example, our determination to provide a handy reference of tools in the margin along with action items gave rise to the use of a wrench as an icon, and that resulted in the photograph we used for the cover. It was exciting to see that our subliminal message of a "tool" targeted our primary readers so well.

Tool

Remember, you want to understand your market before you do your marketing. Otherwise you might be wasting both time and money reaching out to the wrong customers. Your market is based in the definition of your core customer, which should be in your business plan.

That's marketing. The idea in this illustration cost us nothing. The artwork for our cover (which serves as on-going advertising) cost very little compared to the normal cost of display advertising.

Your Own Best Marketer

No one is going to market for you as well as you can. You can go to an agency, but you may end up disappointed. Your results may not be what you want and you will have spent a lot of money on the effort.

Ad agencies are probably not your best bet because you simply can't allocate the financial resources required to hire an agency approach.

We believe the best thing you can do is to learn to understand marketing. It starts with an examination of who your primary customer really is. Once you have that definition in hand, you can begin to catalogue ways to reach that specific market. There are hundreds of ways when you actually ponder it. Most of them won't cost you much, if anything. Pick a good business book for example. Read just a few and you'll learn more than you can implement. Two of Ron's favorites are Customers For Life and The Discipline Of Market Leaders.

If you are monitoring your numbers as we suggested early on, you can measure your

Tool

Identifying your core customer on paper helps you determine how to market to them in a better way. You should have done this in your business plan.

results in cost per contact. That ought to keep you away from the agency approach.

So do you hire a consultant?

You don't unless they are industry savvy. We've done that. We still do on occasion; yet seldom are we pleased with the results.

Tool

You should read all you can about marketing. Create a schedule that will allow you time to do this. It should be part of your tasks as owner of your company. Other things you do now can be delegated if you only look to see how. This research will pay handsome dividends down the road.

On the contrary, we recommend from our experience that you read up on marketing all you can, that you get yourself educated in marketing techniques, that you go to tradeshows and understand how your competitors market themselves. In short, you are far less likely to find significant success, far less likely to salvage millions from your small business if you don't acquire a savvy understanding of marketing. Many mediocre products and services produce good profits due to savvy marketing, just as many brilliant products and services fail because of poor or non-existent marketing.

Your objective is to gain understanding in how to match your product or services or both to your primary customer.

How To Make A Change

In the mid-eighties, Ron thought things were moving along pretty well for his business. He was going through the motions, going to work every day. He had little or no competition and was doing okay. But he wanted a lot more.

One of his competitors had worked for Ron at one time. He was a low-price provider. He bought cheap cars from individuals and sold everything for very low prices. Ron bought his cars at auctions where he had to pay more for them in most cases. The competitor seemed to be doing a lot of volume, but Ron couldn't tell whether or not the man was making a profit.

After awhile, Ron began to get irritated at the number of customers coming in who'd been over to his competitor. They whined when they came to Ron, saying such things as, "Over there, we got it for this amount," or "I can get it for such and such at that other store." Not willing to drop his prices and engage in a price war, Ron decided he would not offer the same products as his new competitor. He shifted to the upscale Mercedes and BMWs for parts. At the same time, he began a nationwide marketing campaign.

Within just a year or two he grew to where more than 60% of his sales came from outside the state of Texas. Another 20% were well outside the Dallas/Fort Worth area. That meant that due to his marketing efforts 80% of Ron's customers were coming to him from outside his local market.

He did this by first identifying a core customer, one that was not a general population customer. Ron didn't have to lower

prices to service this upscale clientele. Instead
he had to provide them with quality parts in
an efficient manner. He decided that his
primary customer worked on Mercedes and
BMWs and found there was a big market for
that nationwide. At that time, he had
virtually no competition for that market. To
find his buyers he went to garages and body
shops nationwide, tracking as much
information as he could. Later, when Lexus
and Infiniti entered the marketplace, they
became natural additions to Ron's product
offerings.

He soon found that certain zip codes were
providing more calls than others. Some zip
codes, in fact, showed very high numbers of
calls per advertising dollar. This became
invaluable information. It was so valuable that
Inc. Magazine ran a story in June, 1994 on
Ron's technique of tracking customer calls.

Tool

*Ask yourself whether
you are the low-cost
provider, the total-
value provider or the
highest quality
provider to your
customer base. You
can't be all three, but
you might be two of
them.*

Analyze Your Approach

In 1993, Fitz opened a new location about
60 miles south of their existing locations, near
Tacoma. Traffic in the Tacoma area made
timely deliveries very difficult. A new facility
at Graham was put in place to provide faster
service to their customers.

DL created a marketing plan that outlined

how they would attract retail and wholesale business in the Graham area. Following the plan, they advertised on the back of buses. They figured all the slow-moving traffic would have plenty of time to look at their ads.

They failed to consider, however, the increasing volume coming out of wholesale shops about that same time. The increase was the apparent result of a good product being served up on a timely delivery.

The back-of-buses campaign was expensive and yet the retail market in that locale did not reflect the gains they anticipated. Retail generally provided fewer hits per dollar spent; the market was too broad. They were broadcasting to everyone by virtue of the bus ads. No primary customer had yet been identified.

As DL and his father analyzed and discussed the situation at Graham, they realized most of the business was wholesale. So they decided to slowly cut back on their bus-advertising budget.

This point should help distinguish the differences between advertising and marketing. They gained business by cutting their advertising budget in half and focusing their efforts on the wholesalers. They redirected that advertising revenue into marketing directly to their target customers, monitoring the zip codes against the returns. They created a customized list of wholesalers within reach. They added new customers by going after them with outside sales reps.

More direct marketing by mail and sales reps and personal contact caused a surge in their wholesale sales. They still served a retail market, but they were no longer throwing money at it unnecessarily.

Interview Your Customers

Tool

Having the knowledge of who your core customer ackually is can help you curb undue expenses and prevent key losses. With a bit of pondering, this knowledge may redirect your efforts in reaching this primary basis of your business.

Here's another brief marketing tip. Isolate your top one hundred customers. Put them down on an exclusive list. Then interview them, go out either personally or through your sales reps. Ask about your competition. Ask your customers what they want or need most. Ask them what pleases them within your service/ product structure and what would please them more. You want them to suggest ways in which you could be of even better service or provide a better product. One of them just might give you a clue you hadn't considered before.

That's marketing. You define the customer. You make sure he knows who you are and what you provide. Then you go after the customer to see what he really needs and what he really desires. If you can, you fill the need, provide the desired service. The return is in part more revenue, which of course you want; but you will also see returns in customer loyalty. It's something you can't buy with advertising dollars.

Once you know who your customer is, you use that information to guide all your decisions. This knowledge helps you determine how many parking places you should put in, how many delivery trucks you really need, and what to display in your showroom. It affects all product and services decisions.

Once In, They're Yours

Charles Tandy of Radio Shack fame once said, "Your most likely customer is the customer who just bought something from you."

With that in mind, Ron held weekend events twice a year where customers could come in and retrieve their own auto parts. Twenty dollars would provide you with all you could carry. Some of Ron's competitors had done that quite successfully by creating $40,000 plus on a 2000-visitor turnout for a weekend.

But Ron thought a greater return was possible. He took a little different tack on the idea. Ostensibly calling it a liability waiver, he made everyone sign in on a log with a full name and address. If they didn't provide all the information, he wouldn't let them on the premises. He spent a lot of money marketing

Tool

Create a list of your top 100 customers and systematically ask everyone of them how you can improve your service to them. Some will give you great insight; others will recognize your effort to please them. You will benefit immeasurably from this effort!

the event, sometimes spending as much as $20,000 to generate the necessary turnout. If he took in $50,000, he was still way ahead. The difference was in what he did with the mailing list he generated from the sign-in logs. Six months later when he did the next All You Can Carry event, he spent only $10,000 which included the mailing to those same people. Six months later he spent only $5,000 and each time the sales increased. Once they've been there, your customers will return if they know you're having the sale. The key is found in letting them know you are having the sale.

Tool

Remember, the best customer you have is the one standing in front of you.

Remember: "Your most likely customer is the customer who just bought something from you." That's marketing, but only if you go after it! Create mailing lists anyway you can. Use post cards to promote special events. Increase your mailing lists every time you host a special event. Tell them on the postcard that if they will bring the postcard with them, you'll give them a dollar off their purchase. That provides them with an incentive to hold onto the postcard. The postcard then becomes a reminder of the upcoming event.

Sometimes Ron would run these events two weekends in a row. The *All You Can Carry* product generally came from cars he was going to crush anyway, not from high-end inventory; so everything he sold under these terms was cash he'd otherwise lose.

Thinking Is Marketing

Because Ron learned so much by doing this, he asked his florist and framing shop owners whether they kept mailing lists of their customers. He was amazed to learn that neither one had such a list despite the fact that they had been in business for years. The more he looked around the more he saw the same symptoms. Small businesses of every variety were failing to obtain mailing lists of customers who'd bought items from them, yet they were complaining about the lack of growth or profitability in their enterprising.

He heard complaints, too, from many of the business owners he questioned. The complaints were about the high cost of advertising. Ron was amazed at how many consistently failed to recognize that their customers were going away every day without leaving any contact information behind.

Customers would buy something, pay for it, and ask for their receipt and leave. And the owner would know nothing more about them, nothing about who they were, where they lived or how to contact them. In order to bring them in again, the owner would have to spend more advertising revenue. Cash flowing out the door could have stayed in many of those businesses had the owners thought to collect data on how to reach their customers.

Tool

Create a database that will allow you to keep track of and communicate with your customers on a mass level, say through a mailing list. If you're not computer savvy, try to record their names on card files or copier labels. They are your direct link to success and you must know how to reach them.

Tool

From where do your customers come? You should know. Make it a point, for at least a few days, to ask every customer who comes in or calls, how they were led to you. Record what they tell you in note form. This will help you make critical marketing and advertising decisions.

There's always a way to achieve this. Reward those customers who are willing to log in. In some cases, as Ron did, you can require them to register, with all the information you need. You may experience a few dissatisfied or unhappy people who complain about your collecting information, but in general you will increase your customer base considerably because you will be able to correspond with them for special events or new product announcements. That's marketing.

We'll give a little plug here for Mike French of Mike French & Company, Inc., 1-800-238-3934 in Seattle. He's shown us that he is more intuitive and less expensive than most competitors, even nationwide for printed materials, especially regarding direct mail promotions. Here's an entrepreneur who's marketed himself well serving a number of national clients as an agency, creative source and a competent print, mail and fulfillment outlet. Further, he offers these serves at prices friendly to small business efforts.

We found him to be an aggressive and practical example of competent marketing. You should try to be like that in your own industry.

Chapter 11

Your Image

How you present your image is important to the subliminal imprint on your customers' memories. Have you got a logo for your firm? How about a standard color theme? If not, it's time to think about your business image and its overall symbol in the public mind.

Say you have a floral shop. Over time, you've learned to identify your primary customers and you've found they really like red roses. Then your logo should be a red rose. Go a step further; paint your floral shop the color of red roses. Hire a muralist to paint the front or side of your building to look like a red-rose garden.

Do you see what we're saying here? The consistency of your visual image becomes an imprint in the mind of your customer. You want that imprint to be elementary because simple images are easier to grasp and remember. A primary color, like red or yellow, files into human memory in such a way that it's easily recalled. Simple cues will call forth a graphic picture quite easily, and that's good for you and your business.

Your logo should be a reflection of your firm. Why are simple graphics used on highway signs? It's so that anyone can follow the directions regardless of their language. We all know to drive more cautiously when we see the warning sign indicating a deer crossing. We all know how a stop sign looks. These images are filed away in our subconscious memory to act as a simple, easily identified language. That's precisely what you want to achieve with a business logo, and precisely what you should achieve by implementing a company theme throughout all the visible areas that greet your customers coming and going.

It's part of an exercise called "branding". It's a business take-off on the western concept of branding a rancher's cattle and horses. In the Old West, it left no doubt about who owned what. It's given rise to our modern day use of logos to establish a simple-language image to help customers and the public at large identify particular services or products with a particular business.

Start the process by simply asking yourself what makes your products or services better than those of any competitor, or what distinguishes your company.

Branding is making your product stand out

Tool

Your logo should clearly communicate that you have what your core customer wants. If it doesn't, consider creating a new logo.

from all the rest of the advertising noise we hear broadcast in a thousand ways every day or that we see plastered everywhere in print. If you're going to be seen, you've got to compete. If you're going to compete, you've got to stand out. The marketplace is noisy. To get business, you need to be not only noticed, but remembered as well.

If you think what you're selling is a general commodity and that it can't be branded, you're wrong. Milk is a commodity and look what Carnation has done with that. Bottled water is a commodity, but look what the entrepreneurs have done with that! Fuel is a commodity, but there are all kinds of brands promoting various attributes of additives. "Put a tiger in your tank," one purports. That's branding. You'll likely see a picture of a tiger on the building and recognize a color theme particular to that product. That's how the idea enters the public mind and why it stays there from one generation to the next.

In his advertising and on his billing statements, Ron adds the phrase, "Ask about our lifetime warranties."

He was attending an auction one time when a friendly competitor came up to him and asked, "I want to know how the heck you guarantee your parts forever. I see that lifetime warranty thing. That's crazy. You can't guarantee parts forever."

Ron replied, "We don't guarantee all our

Tool

Even the most common product-types and services can be branded for distinguishing your business in the marketplace. Just look for those things that make your business different from your competitors.

parts forever."

"Well, your ads say you do!"

"No. Our ad says, 'ASK about our lifetime warranties.' "

"Oh, well I thought you guaranteed all your parts forever."

This is a good example of how an idea enters the public mind. Different people might read the same phrase and remember it in different ways, but here's an example of a competitor who became mildly irritated because he couldn't guarantee his own auto parts "forever." If he had been a customer of Ron's, he might have chosen to come to Ron rather than go somewhere else because Ron offered a lifetime warranty.

If it accomplished nothing else, the phrase advertised the willingness on Ron's part to back up some of his specialized auto parts. Although his customer wasn't required to purchase the extra product coverage, it was offered nonetheless. The idea made Ron's company stand out over other competing companies and helped establish customer loyalty he might not have otherwise acquired.

Stand Out

Branding serves to influence a customer's perception. Doesn't Mrs. Butterworth's syrup just taste buttery and gooood? If you bought a Betty Crocker cake mix, wouldn't you expect it to be moist and pleasing to the palate? That's branding.

Your company name is your brand. It is also your intellectual property. It's good to understand the value of your intellectual property. You sign your signature on checks and important documents. It identifies you as you. Your company name is the same. If someone is trying to mimic you in order to capitalize on your advertising/marketing budget or on your established name brand, you may have legal recourse.

It never hurts to register the company name you've chosen. That carries a lot of weight in a court case should someone challenge your idea. DL came into Fitz as a fourth generation college graduate with the knowledge of how important this could be. He asked his father if he'd ever registered the name they'd been using for 70 years. His father hadn't, and gave his son permission to do so. DL did that and now the brand name can never be successfully challenged in a court situation. It also added considerable value when the company was sold.

You work hard to establish an imprint in the collective consciousness of your customer base as well as in the public mind at large. It's your intellectual property. Preserve it. Protect it.

Action!

Set a date to register your company name as a trademark.

As you grow and take on other locations, it's a very good idea to register with the national trademark office. Trademarks are like patents. A proven history of use is important and necessary. The sooner you register your trademark, the better off you'll be in protecting your brand name. Don't wait until you're a millionaire. Do it early on; then when you achieve significant success, no one will be able to rock your boat-at least in that regard.

Networking

Networking is a great key to opening potential customer awareness of who you are and the nature of the business you have to offer. We're not talking about the fairly new craze in "network marketing." We are talking about how you move through your community in a valuable way for the purpose of bringing relationships your way.

Networking effectively means that you are thinking strategically about the contacts you make. Someone once said that people attract others like themselves. There's another version of that you ought to consider trying: Put yourself in contact with the kind of people you want to attract.

So try to associate with people whose

business you want.

How do you network with people who will send customers your way? Ask to serve on a public board or on a corporate advisory board. Volunteer to work in your trade association. Insight from anyone is a welcome commodity where service is voluntary. When you contribute valuable insight, the ones you've helped will send people you don't know, your way. It's human nature.

Another way to network is by volunteering to speak at business meetings, association meetings and club luncheons, especially those of your customers. You can also join and participate in your local Chamber of Commerce. There are probably more local associations than you would realize. They all meet on a regular basis and most of them are hungry for speakers or articles for their newsletters.

You may not be comfortable speaking in public, but we'll wager that when you realize that speaking in public is really just a form of practicing negotiations, you'll find comfort. The more you do this, the better you'll be at it. The key is not boastful bragging about your accomplishments, but informative engagement of an audience on a subject they should know about: your business or some aspect of your industry.

Tool

Look for opportunities to speak publicly. Though the thought of it may be intimidating initially, you'll gain confidence by doing it. It's not only a great way to market your business, but adds respect to your image as a business person.

Practice Makes Perfect

Think ahead about the people with whom you work and associate, and about the people you serve. That means asking yourself the short and long-term effects or consequences of every major decision you consider. Strategic thinking is a habit you develop. It's something that becomes part of you as you exercise the habit.

Tool

Practice public speaking on your spouse or in front of a mirror. It's worth it. And make notes to keep you on track.

Practice your strategic thinking by putting yourself in situations that cause you to grow. Whenever a given situation crosses the comfort zone of your personal makeup, you've grown a little in a good way. Negotiating is never comfortable. But practiced negotiation is actually quite easy, if not downright fun.

Engage yourself in the challenge. Go and meet it. Stand up and see if you can determine what actually holds an audience and why. You'll find the answer hidden in eye contact. This is true for public speaking, and it is true in negotiation. The reason it is true is that eye contact conveys to others the notion that you are really paying attention. At some point you have engaged your audience by virtue of eye contact.

Don't let go. Hold the eye contact. If you practice this, you'll soon discover that after a time, you'll take fewer notes. Your direction in the speech or conversation will be led by the degree of involvement with those you're addressing.

The value of strategic thinking was brought to light for Ron during his experience with the United Recyclers Group, a limited partnership of 300+ auto recyclers Ron and a few friends created in order to pool resources and address industry issues. Most of the other managers in the group said they learned more about strategic thinking there than they had in any number of years of prior experience running a business.

They never understood, they said, what it meant until they became involved in the organization. The involvement forced them into strategic thinking. The same was true for Ron, as it forced him into deeper levels of thought regarding the unfolding of his business and the industry.

Strategic thinking means contemplating the results of the activity you are doing at the moment. You ask yourself, "What's going to happen as a result of what I'm doing now?" and then "What will happen as a result of that decision?"

Too often we don't consider the outcome of actions we're about to take. This is true in both short-term and long-term developments. Our tendency is more often to think only about immediate benefits, immediate gratification or immediate results. "What can I get now?" might paraphrase the average approach.

Entrepreneurs in small businesses often tend

Tool

Practice thinking ahead. As you develop the habit of strategic thinking, you will realize great benefits in both business and personal life.

to be too emotional with their decisions. Many over-react regarding issues with competitors. Ron has a rule for weighing the upside gain against the downside risk. First mentally define the goal of any decision or action you are contemplating. If it isn't definable, then going with the decision or action is probably not worth the effort or risk. What's the real upside? What's the downside? Your decision, if you pause to define everything, is usually an easy one.

Strategic thinking takes into consideration the repercussions of the decisions we make from day to day. There are enough impediments to success in the business world without creating more.

We'd like to see more managers consider the results before they take the actions. There's nothing flippant about business. It's a serious game. It should be taken seriously and thought should be given to every decision.

Weigh Your Decisions

Measure the results so you can see the consequences. Not doing so is nothing more than allowing bad habits to rule. Weighing decisions and measuring for consequences is creating a good business habit.

In thinking about how to present the importance of learning to think strategically,

Tool

Keeping eye contact is one of the keys to a successful negotiation. Practice keeping eye contact with your customers as well as with your friends and family. Then when the time comes for something big, you'll be ready.

we've come up with a short program. Try it. You have absolutely nothing to lose, everything to gain.

Make yourself aware of the decisions you make during the day. That's the first thing. Just focus on watching the decisions you make as they roll off your lips into reality.

One of the best things you can do is think about the cause and effect of any action you might take regarding the decision at hand.

For example, what's the consequence of refusing to accept credit cards because some customer successfully passed off a stolen card on you? You'll lose more than you'll protect. There will be customers who can't buy because you've chosen not to accept credit cards. Weigh the cost of the decision. You might be losing more money by not accepting cards. You want to look at the big picture, not just one bad transaction.

In another typical scenario, what would be the outcome of your hiring a relative or in-law? Say this person does not have the skills but needs a job. You feel compassion and want to help. What will the consequence be? Can you afford the time to train her? What will be the consequence? Does she show signs of willingness and desire to learn? What will be the consequence?

These are the kinds of questions you need to ask yourself over and over until the asking

Tool

First you define the goal upon which your decision is based. Then you look at the upside and at the downside respectively to determine the potential costs or rewards.

Tool

Consider the consequences constantly. Think cause and effect before every business decision, large or small.

becomes habit. We're presenting these
scenarios to show the diversity of decisions you
make on a daily basis.

Hidden Wealth In Ownership

There's hidden wealth in the dirt beneath
your business. We're not talking about mining
minerals nor are we looking into the skeletons
in your closet. The hidden wealth lies in the
answer to the question, "Who owns it?"

If you have established yourself in business
and intend to stay in business for sometime, you
should attempt to buy the ground and the
building your business occupies. Renting does
not grow equity. Owning does. The value of the
land will likely grow over time. The return on
that growing value shows up when you want
to sell the business. You'll probably sell the
ground beneath it. If not, as in Fitz's negotiation,
you'll lease the ground to the company that
bought your business. Then you're coming out
even further ahead.

If you are able to pass your business on to a
generation or two following your ownership,
the land will be that much more valuable for
those who inherit it or earn the position of
ownership. So if you can't buy the land you're
on, consider moving to a location you can buy.

If you lease or rent for a number of years in

the same location, you are paying for someone else's retirement!

There's greater wisdom in ownership, even though the payment may be a little more than it would be to rent, because ten years down the road the property is going to increase in value. Also, although the monthly payment may be more than rent, your out-of-pocket cash may be less, due to tax advantages you can enjoy. Why not position yourself so the increase is yours and not someone else's?

Ron had several friends who criticized him for paying too much for his land. But Ron reasoned that since the landlord gave him an owner-financed mortgage with a low down payment, he couldn't pass up the opportunity. He paid if off only 15 years later and felt very good about that.

Look at it this way: If you rent over a ten year period, there's a high probability that when the property value goes up, so does your rent. Your landlord rightly wants to maximize his return on his investment.

Ron and DL believe owning is better in the long run than renting or leasing. It's certainly been true for them; so they recommend it. Sacrifice today for tomorrow's gain.

It pays to have a plan that builds your business over a long period of time. Don't go for the quick buck up front. Plant your feet firmly and grow a real business, one that will

Tool

Owning the ground beneath your business is equity in the making. It becomes a powerful tool of leverage when you go for funding your future growth.

have high value for sale in ten, twenty or more years.

Chapter 12

Lead The Way

Leadership is necessary for a successful business owner. Good leaders grow good solid business returns. So if you are not a born leader, how do you become one? Can this trait be acquired?

You bet it can.

Start watching other people you consider to be good leaders. If possible, put yourself under one for a time. Maybe you could entice them to sit on your board of advisors.

There's a reason we need bosses. The reason is that groups of people left on their own without a boss either pick one out of their midst or they fail to go anywhere. Without a boss, most employees work randomly without direction. Without a boss, workers won't set or meet goals. If they do, it's because someone within the group decided to lead or was appointed to lead according to his natural aptitude.

Most of the population in any country is

Tool

Leadership can be learned. Study the qualities of great leaders and you'll absorb some of the attributes that define their skills.

made up of followers. Few are born to be or choose to be leaders. But if you are going to be in business for yourself and expect to succeed at it, sooner or later you are going to have to lead.

People much prefer to be led by strong leaders. Strong leaders are not necessarily dictators nor are they autocratic. The kind of strong leaders we're talking about are generals with a heart.

A Leader Or A Follower?

A leader not only shows willingness to go a step beyond the necessary but also a willingness to sacrifice in order to assist the reaching of a goal. A good leader often works harder, stays later and arrives earlier than any subordinate. A good leader does not flinch at the difficulty or possibility of an outcome. He anticipates the outcome.

He has an unwavering and focused mindset.

A leader accepts surprises as part of the course. A great leader anticipates a path that inherently holds surprises. With that knowledge, he is not shaken when surprises show up. Instead, he responds creatively, courageously, and with compassion. He finds within himself whatever is required to meet the challenge.

A leader learns to work with people who are different from him in personality. He learns to see their talents and incorporate them in a common goal. He learns to inspire by pointing out the mutual benefits of reaching a select goal. He brings the best out of others because in essence he understands them. He understands them because, in all likelihood, he has worked hard at learning how to do that.

We hope you don't miss the important verb in the above paragraph: *learns*. Few have it at the start. Leadership is learned. It's not the topic of our book. It's a book in itself. We're talking about it because your bid for significant achievement cannot happen without it. You'll have to "learn" to delegate. You'll have to "learn" to inspire, to point out, to build up, back up and assist those you've hired into being better than they were when they came on board. You'll need patience and you'll need the upper hand in the knowledge of your industry. If you don't have these things, you'll have to "learn" how to acquire them.

Go look at other leaders. Put yourself in front of people you believe are good leaders and ask yourself what they do that you don't do. What do they do that followers don't do? You'll likely find they are structured, disciplined and thorough. You'll probably also find they have persevering attitudes, common sense and drive.

Leadership might look difficult, but it

Action!

Read at least one business book every 2 months.

doesn't have to be. A leader leads. A follower follows.

Learn How To Learn

How can you help yourself? We've pointed out that leadership is an acquired trait. If you don't help yourself, nobody is going to do it for you.

You help yourself by seeking out answers in areas where you are weak. Educate yourself in your weak areas; start by reading books about those things you feel you don't fully understand. Why accept weaknesses? Overcome them.

If you don't overcome your weaknesses, it's a sure thing that no one else will overcome them for you. If you don't overcome them, you will own, display and exhibit them in everything you do. You will also be tripped up by them, sometimes right at the juncture of critical timing. So why not seek to strengthen your recognized weaknesses from the start?

Do you need a degree? You don't unless you want one. If owning a degree ensures somehow that you will reach a desired level of understanding or accomplishment, go get the degree. In DL's scenario, his father required a degree before he could enter management in the family company. But the degree was not what his father wanted DL to have. It was the means of proving that DL had staying power and drive that could take the company forward. Acquiring the degree under the mentoring of his father, DL also discovered a high level of self-confidence in the fact that he could work his way through any difficulty. The result of the degree in DL's case is that it provided him with not only some knowledge but also the confidence and fortitude to lead a fourth-generation business onto a new level of success.

But you may not desire a degree, and you may not need one in order to educate yourself. Thomas Edison had no education. Howard Hughes had an eighth grade education. Henry Ford never finished the sixth grade. Yet Henry Ford was the creative founder of the V-8 automobile engine. How did he do that? He told his engineers to create one. They said it couldn't be done. He said, "Do it." They went to their drawing boards, worked at it and came back and said it couldn't be done. Henry Ford said, "I didn't say it could or couldn't be done. I said, 'Do it.' " They did, and today many vehicles have V-8 engines.

In people like these we see great and significant things accomplished. Yet they did not have any formal degree of education. The world today is full of examples like this. But every one of these individuals are people who achieve great things and all have common traits. They believe they can do it. They have a vision for what they want to do. They don't give up on it and they often work twice as hard as anyone else. They remain focused until the solution is found.

So when we suggest that you can improve your current circumstance, we're dead serious. There's no limitation other than the one in your own mind.

Go for it! Stand up, clear your head, lay a plan and go for it. Believe that you can do it. Believe that you can do anything you set your heart and mind to accomplish. You will if you don't give up, if you seek out the answers, and if you "learn" how.

Understand that learning anything is possible, but no one else can do it for you. It's entirely up to you.

Tool

Condition your staff to tell you what they really think, not what you might want to hear. You'll benefit more from the truth behind their opinions and so will they.

Work Hard; Work Smart

DL will tell you that he's learned more about how to solve the problems of real life and real business from the employees, associates, customers and his peers than he ever did by going to college. Yes, he did gain value from higher education and he still applies some of those school lessons today. But the real thing learned comes from the experience of life itself in the workplace, pondering the problems, dealing with them and staying on the search for solutions until they are found. Because that's true, perhaps your greatest resource for troubleshooting a problem for a solution is the people around you.

Ron always puts a problem before his managers, even when he thinks he has the solution. He wants the advice. He wants that one thought that might save him from a blunder. He believes in seeking concurrence on significant projects and doesn't want to be autocratic. He's an achiever. Look at that and mimic his approach.

Ron insists work ethic and ambition are more important than a formal education in the realization of achievement and success. Really, it's a matter of personal preference.

Both Ron and DL are saying that nothing should hold you back from improving your situation. You start with yourself and you improve upon your weaknesses by gaining strength from others who are strong where you are weak.

One gained perseverance by sticking it out through school. The other gained perseverance by going to work early and staying later than anyone else until he could take the day off anytime he wanted. They are both saying the same thing. Work hard. It's a key to your success.

Tool

Not a single tidbit of the knowledge we've given you in this book will do you any good if you don't apply it.

Smart work is even better. Think while you work hard. Examine what you're doing. Look for ways to do it better. Study how others are doing what you can't yet do. Apply what you observe. Use the upside-downside questions to test the wisdom of your decisions. You'll grow. You'll change. You'll become stronger, more courageous and smarter in business, and one day you'll recognize that you've found significant success.

No Such Thing As Luck

We wrote this book to show you how to improve yourself in order to enjoy significant success. But you've got to develop the work ethic on your own. The ambition to do so comes from you. No one can do any of this for you.

If you've gleaned even one small bit of useful advice here, the $15 you spent on this book was worthwhile. Reaching for significant success requires you to leverage everything you've learned in these pages as well as information you gather from other sources.

Just about everyone who runs a business or wants more money has gone to some seminar or convention somewhere to listen to a motivational speaker. Most of the time these people come back insisting the seminar or convention was really great. They resolve to do better, to change; but most never do. They may be motivated and they're upbeat from the message they received from the speaker, and many of them will actually do better for a time; but they slip back into the bad habits, the lazy streaks, and the lack of vision. Sooner or later their performance drops off. They are back in the mud again, some seemingly stuck forever.

Tool

You are the only one who can find the passion you need to succeed in a significant way, or to even succeed at all. You are the only one. No one can and no one will do it for you. It's up to you.

This gives us a reason why we should attend the industry conventions. It gives us a reason why we should go to motivational seminars and read the books these motivational speakers often write. Call it rejuvenating your work ethic or recharging your batteries. Call it coming back into focus. Call it anything you like, but do it.

Unless you are an absolute self-starter, you need to refill the tank of your dream when it runs dry. It will run dry if you do nothing about filling it up on a regular basis.

All conventions import some motivational speakers. You can imagine that they wouldn't be hired or on the circuit if they didn't have something to contribute to the way we do business. Go and listen to them. Take in what they say and see what you can apply. There's no danger, no harm. It's all upside; there's no downside.

It all comes around full circle, doesn't it? It comes back to whether or not you choose to develop a persevering attitude, whether or not you find your passion. It's your choice. No one

else can make it for you. You have to make it.
You start where you are; you get off your chair
and you acquire the skills you need to make
the changes that will send your business into a
new climb. The skills won't come to you. You
have to acquire them. You didn't inherit them
either. No one did. Everyone has to earn success,
and anyone who goes beyond the norm does
so through hard work. Vow, as we close, to fill
in the dates on the **Action List** that follows; and
go to work!

There's no such thing as luck. Get it out of
your mind. If you accept the idea that someone
who is successful is "just lucky", you are fooling
yourself and no one else will care. Drop the
judging. Pick up the desire.

Go after it.

Get out there and find significant success.

It's yours if you want it.

A Work Sheet For
Taking Action

Action Step	Goal to start	Completed
1 - *Page 3* *To encourage the proper use of financial statements, schedule your meetings with your accountant once a month....................................*	__/__/__	__/__/__
2 - *Page 4* *Resolve to study your financial statements and operating metrics monthly.................................*	__/__/__	__/__/__
3 - *Page 14* *Analyze your products and services to determine which are the most profitable.............................*	__/__/__	__/__/__
4 - *Page 18* *Have a meeting with your employees in which together you define your core competencies.........*	__/__/__	__/__/__
5 - *Page 23* *Decide who your most credible competitors are and analyze their operations relative to yours for things you can improve.....................................*	__/__/__	__/__/__
6 - *Page 27* *Schedule time to sit down and create an operating and financial plan for the next 12 months...........*	__/__/__	__/__/__
7 - *Page 34* *List some simple personal goals you want to achieve this year, as well as over the next 5 and 10 year periods..*	__/__/__	__/__/__

Action Step	Goal to Start	Completed
8 - *Page 35* *Set a goal today for when you intend to have the information necessary to set a goal for gross sales next month*..	__/__/__	__/__/__
9 - *Page 43* *Define your core customer in writing*......................	__/__/__	__/__/__
10 - *Page 51* *Use an RFP the next time you need a new service*...	__/__/__	__/__/__
11 - *Page 52* *Buy a PDA today*..	__/__/__	__/__/__
12 - *Page 66* *Take your banker to lunch.*	__/__/__	__/__/__
13 - *Page 70* *Order a copy of your credit report today*.................	__/__/__	__/__/__
14 - *Page 71* *Subscribe to a credit bureau alert service today so you'll know when your credit is accessed or when derogatory information has been reported*..............	__/__/__	__/__/__
15 - *Page 74* *Set a goal and prepare a schedule to issue press releases every other month so that you send out six each year*...	__/__/__	__/__/__

Action Step	Goal to Start	Completed
16 - *Page 88* *Set sales goals for your company as well as for each sales person to project over the next 90 days*..	__/__/__	__/__/__
17 - *Page 89* *Schedule at least one sales-training class per month for the next 3 months*....................................	__/__/__	__/__/__
18 - *Page 91* *Set daily sales goals for each salesperson and integrate little ways to reward them for success in front of others*...	__/__/__	__/__/__
19 - *Page 103* *Study your product and service lines to determine whether there are some you could eliminate without losing too much business*..........	__/__/__	__/__/__
20 - *Page 105* *Set a goal to "fix up" at least 2 items or areas of your business next month*...	__/__/__	__/__/__
21 - *Page 106* *When was the last time you cleaned both the inside and outside of your windows? Do it today*..	__/__/__	__/__/__
22 - *Page 112* *Make sure your delivery driver has romotional material to hand out at every stop*...................	__/__/__	__/__/__

Action Step	Goal to Start	Completed
23 - *Page 130* *Prepare and administer an employee satisfaction survey*..	__/__/__	__/__/__
24 - *Page 132* *Review your employees' responsibilities, and analyze how they relate to your company's promises to customers*..................................	__/__/__	__/__/__
25 - *Page 134* *Join the national, state or local association for your industry*...	__/__/__	__/__/__
26 - *Page 145* *Put your 3, 5, and 10 year plans in writing and review them periodically*..	__/__/__	__/__/__
27 - *Page 161* *Create an on-going list of ways to isolate snippets of time and write what you plan to do in them*...	__/__/__	__/__/__
28 - *Page 194* *Set a date to register your company name as a trademark*..	__/__/__	__/__/__
29 - *Page 207* *Read at least one business book every 2 months*..	__/__/__	__/__/__

More Millions

In the six years since *How To Salvage Millions From Your Small Business* was first published, I've written numerous columns on topics of interest to small business owners. Originally, I started writing these columns for *Recycler Magazine*, but the columns seemed to find a following of their own and before long I had other publications requesting to run some of these columns.

The information that follows in this new section consists entirely of columns that I wrote for publications geared to small business owners. I selected these particular column topics because I felt that they best represented my experience and knowledge as a small business owner. I also chose to include them because they are topics that are relevant to a wide variety of business people. It doesn't matter if your business is cars, bars or guitars - the information included here can be applied to virtually everyone.

The bottom line, regardless of what business you're in, is really rather simple: Become more strategic in your approach, and get help when you need it. You will hear me say it over and over again: You don't know what you don't know. The information is out there, and you should never be afraid to ask questions or get help.

I hope the columns that follow will answer some of your questions and give you fresh new ideas on how to make your small business operation more streamlined and successful.

But beyond that, I hope these columns will also make you take a closer look at your day-to-day operations and discover new questions that you need answered. Keep asking questions until you get the answers you're looking for, and never quit looking for new questions to ask. Remember - there is no such thing as knowing too much about your business prospect or customer!

Careers and Job Hunting

Over the years, I've learned a lot about hiring people - and that's helped educate me in what works (and what doesn't) for people who are trying to get hired. This set of columns looks at some of the tips I've learned about getting hired ... and about keeping that job once you've got it.

Resumes and the Power of Networking For Job Hunters

I am constantly amazed at the skills people exhibit when they are job hunting. I know that job hunting isn't something most people do every week, so maybe I should be more sympathetic.

I get at least two requests per month from friends who are looking (or know someone who is) and want me to help them find work.

Email is a powerful tool. When I need to help someone find work, I circulate their resume in my network of business owners, along with instructions to forward it to their friends.

I have never done this when a job offer didn't appear. The list of friends I distribute it to is a few hundred people. Just think about all the jokes and crap that you get that have been forwarded repeatedly. Imagine how much exposure a good resume can get in just a few hours in a network of people with the capacity to hire.

About half of the job hunters who come to me for help don't have a resume! Another quarter have horrible resumes. With so many tools on the Internet to help prepare a resume, there simply isn't any excuse for not having one. Many applicants are younger or looking for blue-collar jobs, and they don't think having a resume is important.

They are so wrong.

When I used to hire a parts puller or wrecker driver for an hourly wage, I always had plenty of applicants. Very few of them showed up with resumes. Who was I most likely to interview first? Of course, the applicant with a good resume.

A good resume is part of marketing yourself for jobs at all levels. It's a simple way to stand out, get noticed, and get interviewed, especially for blue-collar jobs. When few people take the time to apply with one, you can bet your extra effort in preparing a good resume will get you noticed.

Making Sure You Get the Interview:
Resume and Cover Letter Etiquette

The resume isn't the only important tool needed to get an interview. In most cases, an employer gets plenty of resumes in response to an advertisement for a job opening.

What can really make your resume stand out - and get you in the door - is your cover letter.

Before you apply for a position, research the company thoroughly. Your cover letter should discuss your qualifications and show that you have done your homework on the company.

Have someone else check your grammar and spelling, as the cover letter and resume speak volumes about you and your attention to detail. Once you establish your credibility in the cover letter, you can briefly describe how your qualifications match the job requirements.

The trends in resumes are constantly changing, so you will always want to double-check your resume and see if it is consistent with today's trends. There are three common types of resumes: Chronological, functional, and a combination of the two.

•   **A chronological** resume is almost always written in reverse chronological order with most recent employment at the top, listing strong achievements in recent positions.

•   **A functional** resume typically uses functional headings to highlight areas of expertise or specific skills. Functional resumes benefit someone making a career change or an applicant with gaps in employment. Functional resumes highlight areas of expertise and skills, rather than listing recent employers

•   **A combination** resume offers the best of both worlds. Typically, combination resumes begin with skills and accomplishments and then follow with job titles listed in reverse chronological order.

I recently placed an ad to hire an Administrative Assistant. In all, we received more than 300 resumes. I found the combination re-sumes the most straightforward because they highlighted both work history and skillset.

Make your resume clear and easy to read, don't mix and match font sizes and styles. I tossed resumes that were hard to read because of overuse of font sizes and styles.

One other resume tip: Do not embellish or exaggerate on your resume. I interviewed a promising candidate for the AA posi-tion, but some things about her past employment did not add up. Some simple checking revealed that she had lied about her qualifi-cations. We did not hire her.

Employers expect you to tailor your resume to fit the job that you are applying for, but customizing a resume should not in-clude exaggerating your qualifications.

Another tip for sending resumes by email: Use the header to your advantage, reference the job number or position. Make it easy for the person receiving your resume to get it to the right person!

Would You Trade $250 for $8,000?
Plenty of Today's Job Applicants Don't

If you are entering the workforce today, how many times do you think you will change jobs before you retire? A dozen? In fact, Penelope Trunk, a columnist on careers for *The Boston Globe*, estimates that today's new employee will change jobs every two years.

Because it is an important investment, most people spend hours (or days) picking out their next car, but how much time do people devote to investigating their next possible employer?

Certainly choosing the place where you will spend 40 or more hours a week for the next several years should be a decision worth in-vesting lots of time to research.

Having interviewed job applicants many times in my ca-reer, I find that most don't prepare themselves by studying the company where they're applying. With so many resources avail-able online and elsewhere, doing even basic research can put you far above most applicants in an interview.

Think about the last time you were a job seeker. I'll wager

that you started by updating or preparing your own resume. If you did, ask yourself these questions: How much training have I had in preparing resumes? How much do I know about creating a resume that will be sorted into the **must interview** pile?

If you answered *not much* to either question, you should make a smart money investment in yourself.

Before you start sending out resumes, seek the help of a professional resume preparer. Look for the best-qualified person to prepare a winning resume for you. If your new position equates to $10,000 more a year, why worry about spending $250 to make sure that your resume looks sharp enough to get you an interview?

Not presenting your resume in the best possible light can cost you a small fortune. Last week I tried to convince a bright 36-year-old woman who had been laid off from a $14 an hour job in the mortgage industry to ask for $16 an hour. She had the skills and experience to warrant the increase, but her resume sucked because she prepared it herself. As a result, she was struggling to get interviews for jobs that paid less than the one she lost.

I advised her to invest in having her resume professionally done. She said that she couldn't afford it. Assuming a better resume could get her a $2 raise, she breaks even three weeks from her hire date. From then on, she's banking an extra $4,000 a year.

She should have invested in marketing herself to prospective employers with a professional resume, and so should you when your time comes.

I've had a lot more training reviewing resumes than preparing them. From the hiring side of the table, I can report that most resumes I see look like they were created by the applicant. I rarely see a resume that has obviously been professionally written and edited, even when I am interviewing executives. A professionally prepared resume is a smart investment in yourself and an easy way to make the right impression, even before the first interview question.

Remember, only you can make business GREAT!

Learning From *The Apprentice*
Competence Isn't Enough

I read an article recently about one of the candidates in *The Ap-*

prentice, Amy Henry, from Arlington, Texas. She explained what she learned from being on the show and shared her thoughts about entrepreneurship and success.

She observed that competence in the workplace isn't enough to ensure success. I agree completely. We all have employees that are very competent, but for one reason or another, they don't advance very far. Many of these people, I believe, have good technical skills, but that's all they have. Some even have good management skills, and although a plus, even that doesn't ensure maximum success. In today's fast-paced and complex business environment, it takes a full set of skills to get to the top.

Amy went on to say, "You have to embrace more assertive strategies in order to move up. You have to speak up for yourself, feel comfortable about bragging. Embrace high profile appointments, take risks."
This is very true.

Many of you know me personally, but for every one of you who has met me, I find there are many more who know of me. You have heard about me or something that I accomplished.

As most of you know, my dad passed away when I was a senior in high school, leaving me an old VW to keep running, and my step mom threw me out when I couldn't pay her rent. I received little college education, and started a repair business with one employee and an old car. Later, I got into the auto salvage business with 35 parts cars that I had accumulated.

The headline, from my experience, is that almost anyone can achieve maximum success. I am self-taught or taught by a mentor on everything from accounting, marketing and sales management, to private stock offerings and real estate construction, sales and management.

As Amy points out, you have to be assertive. And you have to speak up and be willing to discuss your success. The world is a noisy place, and only those that speak up are going to get noticed. Yes, it offends some people.

Even in the salvage industry, some people resent me because of my accomplishments, self-promotion, and assertiveness. I try to not let it bother me, and you shouldn't either. Every time I issue a press release, or got published somewhere, I send a copy to my bankers, and sometimes to friends. The bankers drop that information into my file, and it always makes my relationship better. How will others know about your accomplishments if you don't tell them?

Amy gives one other tidbit of advice. She adapts by, "…being a strong listener and choosing your battles. If you go out and fight every battle, you will lose most of the time."

Again, I agree. You have to remain focused, and we simply don't have enough energy or hours in the day to do everything, or fight every battle. When I teach clients to use operating metrics, I tell them to pick one that they believe they can change, which will make a real bottom line difference, and work on it. Trying to work on improving too many metrics at once is just a distraction, and creates stress with almost no benefit. In any case, although I don't watch a lot of TV, I tune in for the business lessons taught on *The Apprentice*.

Sales and Marketing

*Running a successful business often comes down to your abil-
ities in sales and marketing. Although these columns were
written with the auto salvage industry in mind - and use that
industry as an example - the principles are applicable to nearly every industry out there.*

How Much Better Than The Competition
Do You Need To Be?

When I speak at salvage industry conferences, I find
that usually one or more attendees approach me after my talk.
They want advice about how to cope with the brutal downward spiral in selling prices for used parts and the increased
expenses of running a recycling operation.

When asked about some of the fundamentals that I've
just spoken about-offering extended warranties, taking steps
to reduce dismantling costs, or putting salespersons on com-
mission-none have been done.

My response is generally the same: You just need to be
a *little* better to beat your competition.
Even more encouraging: Once you make the decision to focus
on beating the competition, the odds of achieving a measurable difference are way in your favor.

Let me share with you why I feel that way.

Imagine that your business has 100 competitors. Consider where most of them are in relation to these four key
thresholds that lead to competitive advantage:

1. **Recognizing that there is an issue** - Most owners and
managers know that they are facing pressure on earnings. Something isn't quite right, but they don't want to devote the energy
to defining the issue precisely. I would estimate that only about
one in four has the willingness to face issues directly. So, out
of 100 competitors, simply recognizing the issue puts you in
better shape than 75 of them.

2.   Zeroing in on the issue and creating a workable so-lution - Now, how many of the 25 competitors left will act upon the insight? How many will invest the time to design a workable solution? Let's be generous and say that half of the remaining competitors recognize the issue and can remain focused long enough to design a solution. Now, of your hypothetical 100 competitors, only 12 remain.

3.   Quantifying the solution with goals, metrics, and milestones - As business owners, we know that implementing a major initiative (such as shifting sales people and delivery drivers to pay for performance) doesn't happen overnight. It takes careful planning and good leadership. It requires sound management and an agreed upon measure of progress. How many of your competitors will do this step effectively? Let's be kind and say half of the remaining 12 get this far.

4.   Executing the plan - Among the six of your competitors that have a plan with measurable milestones to deal with the issue(s) that have been identified, only half, or three, will have the gumption to carry it out. It takes a lot of energy and involves changing key processes. Before you become discouraged about competition, consider that only three of your hypothetical 100 competitors *might* be doing the right things to make meaningful improvements to their businesses.

The very good news: If you can carry out these four steps, you only have to be a *little* better than these final three to win.

You must delegate effectively to make sure that you cross all four of the key thresholds to lasting competitive advantage. If you find you're stuck, get help. It's available, and the cost is small relative to the IMMINENT decline in earnings you will see if you don't constantly innovate, cannibalize your old paradigms in favor of new ones, and change.

My friend used to say I threw 100 changes against the wall every year, and only a few really stuck, but they were real humdingers.

Good Marketing Isn't Rocket Science:
Find A Way to Set Yourself Apart

So many folks ask me to help them with marketing and advertising when I do a consulting assignment. Historically, most recyclers don't spend enough of their revenue on advertising (I recommend at least 1-2 percent) because they have had bad results and don't know what to do. I am always amazed when I see sponsorships of racecars and softball teams touted as effective marketing and advertising.

I am completely self-taught on marketing, and you can be, too. It's not rocket science. If you read a few good books, you will know most of what you need to know. In addition, I used Mike French for my direct mail campaigns; he is a life-saver, as he understands our business so well. Moreover, he designed, printed and mailed the piece. About every fourth job, I got competitive bids, and I don't believe he ever lost a job.

In 1994, *Inc. Magazine* did a nice article on our marketing and advertising at AAA Small Car World. We had a very simple but sophisticated system for tracking results from all forms of advertisements and direct mail, and then tracking and reconciling sales and phone calls. As a result, we knew which mediums delivered the best bang for our buck. (Email me for a copy of that story.)

A good marketing and advertising campaign has to start with a genuine understanding of your customer, your products, and your services, so that you can make sure they are all aligned. For too long, recyclers have believed that anyone that drove a used vehicle was a prospect, but that definition is much too broad.

A sustainable, results-oriented program must include these factors:

- Direct mail, with measured results
- Print and the Yellow Pages (likely only a small amount of Yellow Pages) advertising
- Internet and web presence, with email capability
- Products and services that match your customer and mediums, with a thorough understanding of the desired retail

and wholesale mix
•   Press releases and other methods of networking (many
are free)
•   Focused campaigns for existing customers and pros-
pects.

Charles Tandy (of Tandy Corp fame) once said, "The most
likely person to buy something from you is the person that just
bought something from you." We spend an inordinate amount
of time trying to get new business instead of prioritizing and
focusing on existing customers.
        There are two types of advertising: Brand building, and
selling. Although your brand is valuable intellectual property,
I believe we should spend the bulk of our budgets on selling
advertising. Here are examples of each:

1.   Brand advertising - A flier shows a bottle of Jack Daniel
Whiskey and says, "Reward yourself."
2.   Selling advertising - A flier shows a bottle of Jack
Daniel Whiskey and says "Jack Daniel quarts, $8.99 at Bud's
Liquors, through July 31."

        There are examples; Some URG partners have lever-
aged the URG logo and standards of quality and service into
something that differentiates them from their competitors. I
once wrote an article that discussed branding sand. Your job is
to create the perception (real or not) that *your* products are
better than your competitor's.
        One way we accomplished this over a decade ago was
by offering lifetime warranties. Let's face it; your used alterna-
tor is not very different from your competitor's offering. I once
had an inquisitive recycler ask me, "How can you guarantee
parts forever?" I said, "We don't guarantee them forever." He
said, "Your ads say that." I followed, "Yes, our advertisements
say ask about our lifetime warranties." I am not sure if he understood that our *willingness* to guarantee the part forever
created the perception that it *must* be better.
        Figure out how to differentiate yourself from your com-

petition; then use selling advertising to leverage that into greater sales and profits.

Finding Good Salespeople For
Your Salvage Operation

How do we find good salespeople? First, let's take a SWAG (sophisticated wild ass guess) at defining what a good salesperson is. The following is a rough list of the attributes of an *acceptable* salesperson for our industry:

1.   Sells at least $50,000 monthly
2.   Has happy customers, credits below the median, and writes credits in a timely manner
3.   Has good attendance and a good attitude
4.   Protects our margins by not just selling on price (Pinnacle will track this for you, but it's more difficult in Hollander and AutoInfo)
5.   Is willing to train and mentor other salespeople

Now, how do we get one, train one, and keep one? Where do they come from? I have seen ex-shoe salespersons sell over $200,000 monthly, and others who appeared competent with good attitudes that after a year of training couldn't sell $25,000 per month. I am firmly convinced that they don't have to come from within our industry. If you can, hire a good one from within the industry, and you should of course always consider promoting from within. In all cases, you should have some criteria should in hiring, training and evaluating your salespeople.

If you don't have some written policies, consider putting some together for salespersons. Also, although I have seen strict sales scripting, and no scripting, I am convinced that some folks have the gift needed for this job; others simply don't. (More on how to ascertain that in a moment.) Please read *First Break All The Rules*. This book devotes a whole chapter to why scripting does and doesn't work, and the book will provide useful insight into why some folks have what it takes and some don't. The book is also helpful in understanding how to have happier employees and what that can mean to your profits.

Make sure that you have a good job description, albeit brief, for all new applicants. Some folks use personality testing: I don't have a strong opinion on its usefulness. (Please send me more info on these tests if you know of successes.)

The key (other than making the best hire)? Make sure that you have some reasonable milestones for the new staff, following a week or so of training and tutorials with existing staff. I see folks lingering with weak staff six months after they are hired, hoping that weak their salespeople will get better.

The gift of gab, quick thinking, and other skills necessary to sell will present themselves within days, certainly within weeks of placement. If your goal is $50,000 per month as a minimum level of acceptability, $15,000 in the first month ISN'T GOING TO MAKE IT. In the second month, use $26,000-$35,000 as a minimum requirement. Set your own minimum milestones and make sure the applicant knows those goals, in advance.

I prefer to break the goals into weeks as well. (For instance, if the second month's goal is $30,000, make the first week $5,500, but the last week $8,500) There is simply no reason to keep a salesperson whose sales trend isn't directionally correct. When they stall at $30,000, they can stay there for months, even years.

I recently saw an owner of a new yard put someone in place that they thought could do the job. After about six weeks, it became obvious that this person just didn't have what it takes. The owner got lucky and replaced the weak person with someone who could do the job and had three near-record days in a row. We lose a lot of potential sales fooling around with weak salespersons.

Also, all salespersons should be on commission; the days of salary are gone. This is one of many areas of pay for performance which I help owners with on every consulting assignment.

Making the Switch From Hourly to
Pay for Performance

You have sat in class after class, talked to other yard owners about switching over to paying employees for performance, but you are still paying them hourly. Perhaps you believe that your employees will walk out or that making the switch will seriously disrupt your business.

Just like you, my son and daughter-in-law were slow to change to pay for performance.

They had all kinds of reasons for not making the switch. They wondered why they should revamp their compensation plan when their employees were already giving all they had.

But they were wrong! They still talk about the day they changed to a pay for performance system. It was in 1998, and their delivery driver was having trouble making all the stops.

They found out that was he was going to his girlfriend's house and taking naps while he was on the clock! So they changed his hourly pay to pay for performance (pay per stop), and he quit. They immediately hired a replacement under the new pay for performance plan, and have never looked back. The new driver thought it was great that he could earn more by doing more.

So why risk the change? As owners, we want to have faith in our employees. We can't follow them around and chart their every move. When our employees just can't keep up with the work, we hire more people.

If you are paying your employees hourly, think about how much more productive they might be if they had the right incentives. Switching from hourly to pay for performance will increase your bottom line.

It will increase productivity. Pay for performance weeds out the under performers. You will be amazed by the amount of work your strong employees can do when the proper incentives are in place.

We have helped many salvage yards successfully transition their hourly workforce to pay for performance: Disman-tlers, parts pullers, drivers, and salespersons.

In fact, it's some of the most rewarding consulting work we do, because the payoff is immediate and the ROI is gener-ally exceptional. It's not unusual to see clients reach break even on the change in a week or less. After that, the added produc-tivity goes right to the bottom line.

Leadership and Management

*As you know, there are many issues that affect small business-
es, but good leadership and proper management are crucial
for success. These columns look at some issues in businesses
that often go overlooked.*

Preparing For A Day that We Hope Never Comes

Recently my daughter-in-law lost her mother to a lung disease
that none of us had ever heard of. She passed just 2 ½ weeks
after her diagnosis; before her diagnosis, she was a vibrant,
healthy 68-year-old woman.

My daughter-in-law grew up in this business - her father owned a salvage yard and a crushing business. Her mother
contributed to the family business by paying bills, reconciling
bank statements and performing many of the important behind-the-scenes tasks that kept the business and household
running smoothly.

Most small businesses have someone like that mother.

If something happened to the loved one who takes care
of these behind-the-scenes duties in your business and home,
could you take over their duties? Most likely the answer is
NO. But it's important for every good businessman (and woman) to prepare for a day that everyone hopes will never come.

Prudent business people need to plan for the loss not
only of loved ones, but also for the possible loss of all those
individuals vital to their business. What if you lost your office
manager or accountant? Are you capable of training someone
to take over the job without lowering your level of service?
How much do you really know about all of the tasks it takes to
run your business and home?

Here is a simple way to prepare yourself: Write down
a list of all the duties that each key person performs and then
do them for a week. At the end of the week, you will have a far
better understanding and appreciation for the little things such
as filing, reconciling statements, and other behind-the-scenes
items vital to making sure that your business runs smoothly.

At home, make a list of the duties your spouse performs daily, weekly, monthly, and learn to do them for yourself.

We all sometimes take for granted the people who help us in our business and personal lives. It's human nature. We also believe that somehow our loved ones and key people will always be there to do what they do day in and day out. Not so.

The loss of a loved one often feels unbearable, but it can be made a little less difficult with proper preparation. If you are prepared, you can spare yourself the added worry about what bills are to be paid, when the trash is picked up, and the many other important things your loved one contributes to your home and business.

Estate Planning For Small Business Owners: Lessons Learned From One Mother's Example

My daughter-in-law will tell you that her mother was a very thoughtful person and she understood how difficult her passing would be for those still here. One of the things she and her husband did was to make all of their own funeral arrangements. Although for some this would be difficult, for them it was another way to spare those left behind hundreds of details in a time of deep sorrow.

In our jobs as consultants, we see a great many very successful entrepreneurs who are doing, earning, getting, and achieving. Part of the lesson that my daughter-in-law learned from her mother's example is the value of planning. She did not wait to make her estate plans until she became ill; she planned long before that. Smart entrepreneurs need to make succession plans for their businesses. Smart people need to take the steps to make sure they have given prudent thought to how to leave their affairs in good order.

Fortunately, there are a few easy steps that can really help. Consider designating an executor who can step in immediately to manage your personal and business affairs if you are incapacitated. Consider executing a power of attorney for this person so that your affairs will be in the hands of someone you trust should the unthinkable happen. The power of attorney may be special, limited, or general.

Consider seeing an attorney to prepare a living will and other documents to make your intentions concerning medical care known to your loved ones or your health care providers. Remember the case of Terri Schiavo in Florida: The courts fought for years over conflicting accounts of her end-of-life wishes. Put yours in writing and make sure that all the relevant parties know your intentions.

A surprising number of people are still getting around to doing their estate planning. None of us have the slightest idea as to how long we will actually be here on earth, so get your estate planning done today. If you have an estate plan, is it current? Wills need updating if there has been a change in your estate or family's makeup.

Finally, have a succession plan for your business or have a liquidation plan in your will or testament. Nothing can erase the hurt of losing a loved one, but careful planning now can make it easier for all those who are left behind.

Strategic Planning, Part I:
How Much Time Do You Spend on Strategic Planning for Your Business?

Two things I have learned in working with large businesses over the last decade: Those big guys that we often dismiss as too big and too slow are very focused on doing the things they do best, and they set aside lots of time for strategic planning.

I know that most small businesses owners prize their ability to move quickly and improvise, but there are good reasons large companies invest so much in strategic planning. Before we dig into those, ask yourself these questions:

•   Do you have a detailed written plan of the initiatives that you plan to undertake this year?
•   Do you have three new ways to attract customers that you are planning to try this year?
•   Have you set aside time to evaluate where you could make changes to lower costs over the next 12 months?
•   Do you have a written plan to improve your operations so that you can find and hire excellent employees?

"But, Ron, I can't do all that strategic planning and run my business, too!" No doubt, entrepreneurs are the busiest people on the planet, but failing to make time for strategic thinking costs more in lost time and lost profits in the end.

In the absence of sound written strategic planning, owners and managers have the course of their business days dictated to them. They drift when they could be doing the few things that would be most crucial in the long haul. Of course, events play a role in the course of everyone's day, but the entrepreneur that has done sound strategic planning can see how to position the business to take advantage of them. This operator is working on the important initiatives, and he or she is ready to ask, "How can I use this circumstance to reach my goals sooner?"

The non-planners can only respond to events and hope for the best.

Here's one more thing to consider as you decide whether to invest time in strategic planning: Most of the small businesses you compete against won't make a written strategic plan this year. The point: You will be surprised at how little time you have to invest in strategic planning to get past competitors who don't do any. Make the time, make the plan, put it in writing and measure the results.

Because most small businesses do not have a written strategic plan, they do a little of this and a little of that. Their initiatives don't work because they're poorly prepared and executed. Often a business that has no strategic plan does not know which initiatives to undertake so they try too many.

Maybe skipping the strategic planning worked a decade ago, but it won't work in today's global marketplace.

Strategic Planning, Part II:
The Big and Easy Way of Strategic Planning For Your Business!

In the last column, we discussed how most small businesses just don't make the time to do strategic planning. As a result, they don't grow as fast as they otherwise might, and they are always in a response mode, not ready for future conditions. Many big businesses have a systematic method for analyzing future initiatives, quantifying their value and choosing which ones to undertake.

I learned this method after I sold my business to Ford almost a decade ago, and I've seen it used successfully many times in dealings with investment bankers and other stake holders in the businesses that I have managed or consulted for. Recently, I shared this method with a few small business owners. They were thrilled because this tool makes strategic planning much easier.

I'd like to share it with you. It's called "big and easy analysis." It's simple and it works.

Take a white board or sheet of paper and divide it into four sections by drawing a cross on it. The cross will be labeled with two word pairs (*Small-Big*) and (*Easy-Difficult*). Label one end of the horizontal line Small and the other end Big. Label one end of the vertical line *Easy* and the other end *Difficult*.

Now number each initiative that you are considering as part of your strategic plan. As your planning group analyzes the value of the initiative, place its number in quadrant that corresponds to how difficult or easy it is and how big or small the value of the initiative is to your business.

At the completion of the exercise, you should have all of your initiatives mapped. The tool gives you a clear way to spot the initiatives that are easy and have a big impact on your results. You will likely want to start with those big and easy initiatives and then cherry pick from the others.

You can do this analysis alone, but you'll only get a fraction of the value. The help I offer business owners is to arrange for them to do the analysis with a small group of fellow business owners who are not competitors. The five or six-member groups act as a brain trust and analyze initiatives for each member in succession.

It's powerful because you can tap the wisdom of five other business owners in creating your strategic plan. Perhaps one of the other members of your brain trust has tried something similar to an initiative you're evaluating. Tapping your team can greatly improve the chances of hitting on an initiative that makes money.

A brain trust is a success when each member leaves with a much better plan than could have been created alone. Tapping into the collective intelligence of a brain trust is a great way to make sure your view is objective and your priorities are dead on.

These strategic planning sessions allow business owners to write a strategic plan in an environment where they are undisturbed and in the company of peers motivated to help promote mutual success. Contact me if you are interested in attending such a brain trust planning session or feel free to use the tool on your own.

Is More Money All You Need to Make Your Business Great?

I get so many calls from folks who insist that their only problem is that they need more money. Read my lips: "If your only problem is that you need more money, then you don't have any problems." This is true in almost all cases I have seen. Trust me; there is PLENTY of money out there. The banks NEED to loan it. Investors are sitting on the sidelines. (However, that could change in coming months.)

I do believe that you *think* you need more money. It's a battle, day after day: trying to buy enough cars, pay bills, etc. Getting more money without solving the fundamental, underlying problems is "Ron's watermelon story."

A farmer is bringing in watermelons from Mexico where he gets a great deal at 80 cents each. He sells them for 78 cents but, mysteriously, is always broke. When asked about it, he snaps, "I need more money to buy more watermelons."

I have seen it over and over. A recycler gets a new loan, or a line of credit, and then runs it up to limit. Sales spike temporarily and then level back off at previous levels. But now, there is new debt!

The main reason some recyclers *think* the whole problem is money: <u>profits and cash flows have deteriorated</u>. They have been declining for years, but it's subtle, and we can't or don't want to recognize it.

Other underlying reasons (in some semblance of order) are these:

1.   Too many employees - It's the number one poison. If you aren't doing at least $15,000/month per employee, you have too many. Many have a third too many!

2.   Too many brokered parts, not enough of your own inventory - If you are brokering more than 10- percent of sales in most cases, the $15,000 (No. 1) is out the window.

3.   Not understanding the true cost of goods, with period correct statements - Also, it's critical that you project sales at time of purchase. Remember, as my good friend Jim Counts says, " We don't buy cars; we buy sales."

4.   Lack of pay for performance - Come on, folks; many of your peers started paying their salespersons on commission over a decade ago, paying dismantlers by the car, drivers by the stop, and parts pullers and order fulfillment personnel based upon their performance.

5.   Failure to understand how much their current computer system is handicapping them - It's unfortunate, but you don't know what you don't know. Sounds silly, but it is so true. Just minor advances in being able to price your parts, inventory better, buy just a smidgen better, (the list goes on and on) can save or make you thousands every month, and the cost isn't $20 per day for a newer system, amortized over three years.

6.   Failure to plan - Very few folks have anything resembling a plan that includes operational and financial goals.

7.   Failure to get help - There are lots of peers, associations, and folks to help you out there.

I always say there are four hurdles to success. Who will get over them first - you or your competition?

First, you have to realize that things are tougher. Everyone is getting that one. Second, you have to figure out what is wrong. Third, decide on a plan to improve. Fourth, execute the plan.

Sadly, many folks don't get much past the first hurdle. In spite of this, those who are paying attention are doing very well. Don't let anyone tell you that it's bad everywhere or that it's OK to do poorly because everyone else is. In every region of the U.S., there are folks doing well. Trust me when I tell you that *some* of your competitors are doing well.

Finding Your Niche: A Lesson from Sears and Montgomery Wards

I believe recyclers have tried to be too much, for too long, for too many. We have tried to be retail, wholesale, and everything in between. We have tried to handle too many parts on too many types of vehicles.

We think that anyone who drives a used car must be a prospect.

Although this approach worked 10 years ago when we had 25 percent cost of goods and very little competition, it doesn't work today in most markets.

The customers have too many choices, *other* than used. They can buy new parts, rebuilt parts, or even trade in that old or damaged car on a new or newer car with zero percentage financing and a low payment.

Many years ago, two department stores mailed one-inch thick catalogs to what seemed like every person in America. Both companies, Sears and Montgomery Wards, have closed their general merchandise catalog divisions. Sears still publishes some catalogs for specialty items, like tools.

Before you choose your customer niche, consider, these questions: Do you want to be the low cost provider (Kmart)? Or do you want to be the high value provider (Wal-Mart)? Or do you intend to become the highest quality and price provider (Nordstrom's)?

You can't be all things to all people. I prefer the high value formula. No matter which category you choose or create, it will mean not doing business with some customers who fit into other categories.

Are you going to do import or domestic? Or only a certain make? Or many makes but certain years? Perhaps your niche is mechanical parts or collision parts.

After you choose your niche, look at each of your products and services and tailor them to fit that group. For instance, deliveries may not be important if you are primarily retail. Corrosion warranties won't be important to mechanical customers. Every time you consider adding a new product line or service, think about how well it fits your chosen niche.

Do a full cost-benefit analysis of any new product or service you are contemplating. We once asked our salespersons to generate three ideas in writing concerning how we could improve our sales. One of the ideas was to do two deliveries per day into a given area. Now, to do this, we would need another truck and driver, but I was willing to do it if it would generate enough in additional sales.

Our Pinnacle system was able to measure exactly the number of stops daily into the given area. We went back and generated reports showing that we were currently making 16.1 stops per day in that area. I then put together a mailing campaign for that area, and mailed a postcard every week touting two deliveries per day.

Of course the customers liked it, but the real question was, would they place additional orders because they were getting a second delivery? At the end of 90 days, we re-measured. The deliveries averaged 16.2 stops and our average invoice amount was unchanged. No more double deliveries.

We did this cost benefit analysis before we made the change permanent, and we decided in advance how to measure the benefit to us. When possible, try to agree how you will measure this in advance. Based on competitive issues, some markets might need two deliveries, but the cost benefit analysis showed that we were not getting much in added business for the added expense.

In Business, is Bigger Always Better?

Bigger *can* be better, but many times it simply isn't. First, you have to make several decisions:

• Do you *really* want to be bigger, with the commensurate problems?

• Are you willing to tolerate more mediocrity that will inevitably come from having more employees?

• Are you willing and able to hire employees who have the skills that you lack to get you to the next level?

• Do you have what you deem to be the appropriate mix of personal and business time, and will being bigger effect that mix?

• Will your facility and credit lines (or internally generated capital) accommodate the growth?

Many say that getting bigger will allow greater synergies that will translate into greater sales and profits. Don't believe it. Although it is possible, it's elusive at best. Getting bigger at one location is *much* better than acquiring another facility.

My recycling friends used to ask me how I could manage six locations and 140 employees, when they couldn't seem to keep up with one location. The key, at least for me, was in maintaining good operating metrics and surrounding myself with really good people. If you aren't currently gathering the metrics and studying monthly financial statements that accurately reflect true monthly income and cash flows, don't even consider getting any bigger. Many operators have accountants who don't know how to treat cost of goods and other special recycling issues to give an accurate period correct income statement.

The same friends said they couldn't hire 20 good people, much less 140. If you have weak employees, it's your fault. You either made bad hires, continued to tolerate them, and/or haven't provided the proper training, structure, discipline, and leadership needed. Start being accountable for weak employees; you are the only one who can change this pattern.

I personally know and consult many small yards, with $50,000 to $125,000 in monthly sales, which are making more than 20 percent net profit. On one million in sales, they will

make $250,000 this year in profit. They are doing great and
don't want to lose profits by getting bigger. It's not uncommon
to see net margins below 10 percent in larger operations, even
below 5 percent. *But*, 5 to 10 percent of a big number can be
many more dollars that 20 percent of a small number. You will
have to decide if it's worth it.

A wise friend once told me, "If inventory plays a big
role in your business and being bigger doesn't reduce the inventory cost, there is no incentive to be bigger."

Clearly, there is a time at which this is important, and
you reach a point of diminishing return. A lot of factors drive
such a point, but *really* big, like millions per month, could
easily be past that point. An operation spending millions per
month on inventory is probably paying just as much as the
yard buying 40 cars per month; so 50 cents of every dollar
earned is spent the same way for each operation. That only
leaves 50 cents to carve out a profit and a competitive edge.

The desire to get bigger is endemic to all of us, generally speaking. Boaters have "one footitis," and recyclers always
want later model salvage.

Do what's right for you; don't get bigger just for the
sake of getting bigger or because your competitor is bigger.
Choose your customer niche, understand your core competencies, and execute against a well-made plan.

Getting What You Want from a Vendor:
The Power of RFPs

Does it seem at times that you have trouble defining a new
service or product on which you want a vendor to give you a
bid (i.e., an advertising campaign, new delivery truck, new
phones or phone service, or maybe pallets for the shop.)? In
addition, after you receive the product or service, ever get
something that isn't quite what you wanted or ordered?

Imagine the vendors' frustration with trying to read
your mind when they furnish their quote for services. Tally up
the time that you spend clarifying specifications with each
vendor.

We learned to use a RFPs (Requests For Proposal) as

part of purchasing any big-ticket items. In addition to getting more accurate bids and reducing the time to gather bids, we also received another big benefit from using this purchasing method.

Creating an RFP required us to define much more clearly the product or service that we wanted. We became a smarter and better customer by preparing an RFP.

On a new phone system, for instance, there are a million features and types of systems. What are minimum features that you must have in the system? You will be surprised how often you can't answer these questions clearly without doing the kind of thinking that an RFP makes you do. How can a vendor for telephone systems read your mind?

How many cordless units will you need? How many lines will be funneled through the system, and how much voice mail capability will be needed? After you have a basic configuration in mind, circulate it to key users in your company, and you will probably get significant comments that will help you refine the request before releasing it to several vendors.

Another approach is to release your tentative specifications to a single vendor and then refine it based upon the information that you get from your initial conversations before distributing the RFP to other vendors. By the way, even if you aren't going to get competitive bids, the vendor that gets it first will *think* you are getting bids and will sharpen his pencil on the first presentation.

One of three things will happen when you prepare the RFP:

1.   You won't be able to define the item and/or reconcile it to your needs and goals.
2.   You will define it so well that it is overwhelming, and you will need help or can't even move ahead.
3.   You'll define it so well that you get good competitive bids, and the specification becomes a tool for reaching your goals.

Vendors are your friends, and you need a good team of vendors just as much as you need good employees. If you can't pay them on time, call them. Never avoid them, and always be up front with them. Vendors will help you solve problems with your customers also if you have nurtured a good relationship.

Why Do Some Salvage Operators Thrive When Others Barely Stay Alive?

I have consulted for several yards this year and have been thinking carefully about what the common threads to weak performance are. It is curious that some folks in our business are doing *really well* (15 to 25 percent net profit), but others are barely scraping by.

These reasons that some folks aren't doing well aren't speculation. They're based on my recent experiences consulting for some struggling salvage operators:

1.   **Failure to change** - I know right away when I visit a site whether or not significant progress is going to be made. At least 50 percent of the time, I hear a lot of defensive posturing and reasons why what they are already doing is right. Even when I explain that I have seen their situation many times before, they won't make a change. Most folks think their problems are unique, but I see the same problems over and over in my national consulting practice.

2.   **Too many employees** - This is the single biggest problem. Most of the time I hear all the reasons why this employee can't do this or that. If you aren't doing at least $15,000 per month per employee, you have too many employees.

3.   **Unresolvable family issues** - Dads (and moms) that won't get out of the way and turn the business over to the next generation. Sometimes the creators of a salvage business have unreasonable expectations on value, and/or unwillingness to recognize that new blood (and energy). It's difficult, but I hope I will recognize when it is time to move on and sell or pass on the business *when I am at the top*. Many yard owners passed the top some time back, but they are stubbornly waiting for those days to return.

4.   **Unwillingness (or inability) to use the computer** - The power of the information in our computers is unbelievable.

About 10 percent of the sites that I visit are making good use of the tools that their systems provide to manage their businesses. Many want to know the advanced techniques or secrets of information-driven management, but they aren't using the basic tools they have effectively.

5.   Unwillingness to get help - I talk to lots of folks that are struggling but say they can't afford help. It is unfathomable to me. I always tell folks that they will get these costs back in a day or so on just one or two of the many ideas I (or someone) will give them. There are lots of folks out there spending good money every month on recurring expenses that a consultant could help them dramatically lower. In 1987, when we had one of the worst months ever, I installed the Auto Info computer system. Within months our business had picked up, not because of the computer, but because we were open to getting the right tools and systems in place to improve our operation.

6.   Work ethic & sense of urgency - Where did it go? My friends and employees (and even my clients) will tell you my sense of urgency is hard to satisfy. Do it yesterday!

Will You Compete in Today's Tougher Market Place?

It seems that everyone who consults with me has concerns about his increasing cost of salvage. Most folks aren't computing their monthly cost of goods sold (COGS) properly, so they don't see this problem right away.

They do see one problem, however. They are having trouble buying enough cars because they run out of money in any given period. Now, to varying degrees, operators have always run out of money. When we bought $25,000 worth of cars monthly, it seemed we were broke. And when we bought $1,000,000 monthly, we were broke too. But it is worse than ever, and it seems to go on month after month. This is very dangerous, as fewer purchases lead to one of two things:

1.   Reduced sales, as our wagon gets emptier and emptier

2.   Increased brokering of parts, which makes our margins terrible

Intuitively, you know your COGS is increasing. Please understand that if your COGS increases one percentage point, unless you trim other costs by the same amount, you lose one point of profit. It hasn't been uncommon to see COGS increase 10 points in the last few years. Some (but very few) folks have actually trimmed their labor costs or other costs by that or more, and are doing quite well.

Most of us, however, aren't reacting that well. I always show my clients how to install pay for performance and re-evaluate their complete employee roster in order to make the required improvements. Remember, you should be selling at least $15,000 per month for every employee (and most of those sales should be from your stock, not brokered parts), and some efficient operations are now achieving $20,000 in sales per month for each employee.

The need to rely on our inventory management system for the right information has increased dramatically. We need our systems to tell us how to price, and what we need to buy, and what we can pay for it. It's a little-thought-of phenomenon, but "you don't know what you don't know." Many folks think they have the best because they have never had anything else. If your system won't give you the tools to *automatically* price your parts based on supply and demand, and it won't tell you *automatically* which vehicles to buy, and what to pay for them, and then which parts to pull or leave on the car, then your competitors are getting ahead of you by using better tools.

The coming years are going to be tough for those that refuse to change; changing includes increased use of computers with better software. This ranges from our inventory management system to our ability to email and process images, analyze complex budgets, etc.

It means that employees will need training. I am always amazed at the willingness of yard owners to spend big money on new wreckers and forklifts, but not on upgrading technologies (even though better technology makes us money every day). I am convinced that our industry will continue to have fewer and fewer recycling sites. Falling by the wayside won't be the result of consolidation (all that does is make those who are thinkers better operators). Those that fail will do so solely because they didn't take the necessary steps to be competitive.

The bar has been raised. Will you compete?

Turning an Auto Recycling Yard Around in 90 Days

Recently I had an assignment from a large insurance company that had purchased an auto recycling yard. The company had purchased the recycling yard three years earlier and sales had steadily declined from about $80,000 per month to $40,000 a month average. They bought this yard, wanting to experiment with disposing of their salvage through a salvage yard, instead of through salvage auctions.

They decided at the beginning not to purchase vehicles, but to supply the yard with totaled vehicles they received after settling claims with their customers. They would re-build some or sell as is, and part out the remainder. The problem was their inventory supply was not matched to their customer demand and so sales declined. (They made the mistake of thinking that their claims and total loss vehicles should track with the vehicles their recycling customers would be driving). Of course, they also had too many employees, poor management, and no systems.

When I received the assignment, their average monthly sales were $40,000 per month with about $20,000 per month in re-built vehicle sales and about $20,000 a month in parts sales. The cost on re-built vehicles was over 50 percent and they had eight employees. Expenses were running around $44,000 per month. It didn't take but a few minutes to see they had negative cash flow. Also, if you allocated the employees, with, say, two handling rebuilders and six handling parts operations and sales, they were selling about $3,500 per employee. Remember, the goal is $15,000 to $20,000 per employee per month, and much less than that will not provide a positive cash flow or profit.

After three years of this negative cash flow drain the insurance company decided they wanted to sell the recycling yard and get out of the business. The problem was, no one would want to purchase a yard with negative cash flow. They hired autosalvageconsultants.com to come in and improve operations to get cash flow positive, so they could find a buyer.

I found no systems in place, and the yard was a filthy mess. When a part was sold, someone simply got the vehicle, took it to dismantling, removed the part and returned the vehicle to the yard. I implemented a cradle-to-grave system in the back of the yard for dismantling. Once the proper systems were installed, the process flow corrected and the yard cleaned up (about four weeks), I reduced the staff from eight to five.
The yard was then re-inventoried, and I sold cores, surplus inventory and scrap. I sent out a direct marketing piece (thank you, Mike French!) to wholesale customers and installed a purchasing plan based on customer demand and pay for performance.

Within two weeks after pay for performance was installed, one salesman quit, bringing our staff down to four. Salvage sales increased to $25,000 the first month, a small improvement, but with only four employees, cash flow was getting better.

The second month was much better with parts sales of $42,000. By the third month sales were up to $45,000 and we had a positive cash flow. Keep in mind all of these sales were used part and warranty sales with a cost of goods of about 35 percent, and total expenses were reduced to around $20,000. In this period, no new cars were purchased or sent from the insurance company. (They had cut off all cars.) In the third month, we started buying cars at the local salvage pool, based on customer demand.

During the fourth month I was able to sell the yard for the insurance company and net them a good price, a little more than they had paid for it a few years earlier. In the two months since the sale the new owners have continued with the systems I installed, and installed The Pinnacle Yard Management System - and they are now producing $70,000 a month in sales.

I see these same problems over and over in my consulting assignments. I always find excess employees using bad systems (usually no systems), weak or non-existent financial and operating goals, and a lack of accountability. The lesson here for all small businesses: You don't know what you don't know (think about it), so surround yourself with others that can help and stay focused.

Tax and Finance

Few topics get as much attention - or are as important to small businesses - as those involving taxes and finance. Since I get so many questions about this subject, I've written about it often. Here are a few columns looking at some of the different aspects of this topic.

What Does It Take To Start A Successful
New Business?

I get lots of calls and emails from folks who want to start new businesses.

Opening a new business is not as hard as some people suppose, so long as certain things are done up front. The keys to opening a successful business are to devote ample time to planning and to get expert advice at the outset.

Investing time and money in planning a start-up is like investing in an architect to draw your home plans. It costs 1-2 percent of the capital that you'll devote to the project, but it saves you from making costly errors down the road.

I saw two folks start small salvage businesses this year that faltered. They didn't begin with clear-cut plans. They thought auto salvage was as simple as buying cars and selling parts.

Without having operational or financial plans and without goals or benchmarks, they made it nearly impossible for themselves to succeed. One of these owners was a veteran of the industry with years of successful sales experience. Unfortunately, sales experience isn't enough to create a successful start-up.

They didn't seek expert help at the outset or even when things weren't going well. Both lost in excess of $100,000 in their small operations.

On the flipside, I would like to share the stories of four recent winning small business start-ups. Except for one, all of these small business owners had zero industry experience in the fields in which they started businesses.

Some were smart; some were not as smart. Some had better attitudes than others, but all shared ambition and a healthy desire for success with varying degrees of maturity. One was only 20; another was 48.

What did all four have in common? All four sought help. All four had business plans with fully developed operating plans and financial targets with written goals and benchmarks.

These four started with sophisticated and refined systems that allowed them to run with the right number of employees. They all got SBA loans and had $50,000 to $75,000 of their own money.

All four made a profit in the first 12 months and are doing well, although they are working hard and still drawing only modest salaries.

All four spent about $5,000 developing their plans with outside help and consultation. All four have solid foundations to create businesses with $40 to $60 thousand in sales per month and the systems in place to net 15 to 20 percent profit on those sales.

In other words, all four should make at least $100,000 annually from their small businesses.

The moral: Spend time with an architect before you begin to pour concrete. Have a conversation with a qualified small business consultant to help draw the proper plans for your small business. An investment in sound planning is the smartest first step to building a successful small business.

What is my Salvage Business Worth?

My comments here are very philosophical general in nature, but because I get so many inquiries on this topic, I thought it might be good to discuss it.

I have been hired many times to help determine the value of a yard (not including real estate), in cases including contract disputes, tax cases, condemnations, assisting buyers and sellers.

I have NEVER heard of a wrecking yard (not including real estate) sell for more than one times annual sales, and most often much less. Typically, the sales price for the business is a multiple of earnings (about five to six times its earnings), which need to be legitimately recast to solve errors. Another method is to use the value of the assets. An operation with significant upside can be worth more than five times its earnings. It's funny, most sellers are "just turning the corner on earnings," and see significant upside, even though they have been there decades.

In asset discussion, the value of used parts inventory always comes up. Typically, it can't be worth more than about four months sales (from that inventory, not including brokered parts or car sales).

The earnings used for the multiple must include fair market value rent (which will drive the land value), and compensation for the owner.

The land may be worth more for other uses, and if so, sell it for those uses and close the yard. Also, a typical well-run yard shouldn't need more than 10 acres (many do well with three to seven acres), so I suggest you sell the yard with the land currently being utilized, not to exceed 10 acres, and sell rest of the land to another user who can pay top dollar. No need to buy a shopping center to get a store, from the buyer's perspective.

The land value for the wrecking yard should be driven by the rent payment being made, using a 10 percent or so return on investment. A typical real estate investor will want a higher return due to environmental risk. Obviously an ex-operator could settle for less of a return, as they are more comfortable with the risk. So, your P&L should show the rent, before net earnings. If the rent is say, $3,000 a month, or $36,000 per year, on a triple net lease (where the tenant pays insurance, taxes and utilities), the land is worth $257,000 for the yard use (give or take some, but not much). If you aren't paying yourself enough rent, why not?

If after rent, ($36,000), and adequate compensation to owner (at least $50,000), you still have earnings, of say, $35,000 (10 percent of sales), the business is worth a maximum of $175,000 (five times earnings), and the land is worth about

$250,000 based on the rent being paid. If the rent isn't market rate, or there has been significant development in the area, the land could be worth more of course, perhaps much more. Obviously if the earnings are more and can be proven, the business could be worth more.

My experience is that owners hardly pay themselves anything, and rent isn't being paid, or is not at market rates, and if they were, the earnings are negative, which means the whole enterprise is worth commensurately less.

Ninety percent of people that contact me are unrealistic about the value of their business. Their savior is that their land is worth more for other uses. If you are looking to sell your business, be sure to find out what the land is worth - it may be time to close or move the business and realize the value of the land.

Measuring Performance: Where Do Your Profits Really Come From?

Understanding financial statements and operating metrics are key to your success as a businessperson. If you're going to prosper, you simply must use and understand these tools to know where your profits are really coming from.

First, financial statements. You have to get them monthly by the 15th. These have lots of information, and they can certainly be intimidating if you do not have a financial background. Start a little at a time. Pick a few items to study and focus on, like towing expenses and brokered parts sales. Study them relative to prior months and understand what they mean to your profit picture.

Any good consultant, accountant or advisor will ask to go over your financials with you. A few suggestions can easily make a big difference for your bottom line. When I do consulting assignments, I am always amazed by the number of accountants who don't understand our business and who deliver statements that don't give the owner good information.

Make certain your financial professionals understand salvage. Remember, get your financial statements monthly and spend at least 30 minutes reviewing and comparing them to prior periods.

Second, operating metrics. I touched on these last month but didn't have enough room to discuss them in any detail. They are more fun to develop and use than financial statements, and they can be even more valuable. Again, gather the information monthly and study them by the fifth or so of the month.

Some key operating metrics:
- Total number of employees
- Number of salespersons
- Number of dismantlers
- Number of purchased vehicles, total dollars, average dollars
- Number of days to break even on vehicle purchases
- Total dollar amount of net part sales, core sales, warranty sales, repairable sales, scrap sales
- Cars dismantled per total employees
- Cars dismantled per dismantler (Count all employees involved in dismantling, stocking, cleaning. This should be at least 1.5; 2.0 would be great. Remember to count ALL employees involved in the process.)
- Sales per month per employee (If you aren't at $14,000 or more, you are probably not profitable.)
- Number of invoices per salesperson
- Sales per salesperson (This should be at least $40,000; I have seen as much as $225,000.)
- Percent of credits to sale (This is affected by how and when credits are written.)
- Percent of brokered parts (My bias is toward less.)
- Number and amount of warranty sales per salesperson

You will be intrigued the first month you gather these numbers, but you will really start getting meaningful information by the second month because you can watch for trends. Try to compare your metrics with a friendly competitor, if you can. Any good consultant will have some idea how you measure up on the metrics compared to other recyclers. With this information in hand, reconciling it to the financial statements as needed, you will *really* know where your profits are coming from!

Cultivating the Right Banking Relationships

In this book, I devote an entire chapter to banking relationships. When I started out in business, with one employee in a 10-by-20-foot portable building, which was financed, I quickly learned that I would have to use someone else's money to grow my business because I had none.

I learned quickly how to manage my credit and how to survive with minimum cash flows. There is nothing philosophical about this; it is just plain old bootstrapping. Here are highlights and tips from the chapter on banking.

Managing your credit
•   Make sure you don't allow inquiries into your credit file unless they're absolutely justified. Many vendors will routinely do these; they lower your credit score.
•   Find a community bank where you can have a true relationship. I don't care what the advertisements say; the large national chains can't accommodate you unless you are extremely small (needing less than $100,000 for cars, land and equipment), or very large (needing over $3m). You need a lender that wants to understand more than your credit score.
•   Obtain and review your credit report ASAP, and subscribe to a credit watch service. I was recently a victim of attempted identity theft, and, without a watch service, I could have been in big trouble.

Planning for and communicating with the bank
•   I know it's hard to do a monthly business plan for the next year or two, but you need such a plan to help you be successful and have something to execute against. Preparing such a plan will help you think about the fundamentals of the business. It's OK to present the banker with a less aggressive plan. *Always present the bank with a plan you can exceed, regardless of what you use internally.*
•   Make sure you talk regularly with your banker, if only for a minute. Don't wait until you need a loan to contact your

officer. If your banker isn't taking you to lunch twice annually, find another banker.

• Don't be too aggressive on interest rates. Someday you will be gold plated, but then they can't make money on you. I always said that I wanted the banker to say, "He's one of our best customers, and we make good money on his business."

Always have a backup plan, and, when possible, maintain two banking relationships. The bankers will push back slightly, but it keeps them on their toes and assures that they won't take you for granted.

I have helped quite a few recyclers with SBA loans and was one of the first to be able to explain inventory valuation and cost-of-goods issues well enough for a banker to understand and be comfortable with them. This allowed me to borrow using my inventory for collateral. You must learn these issues and be able to talk about them to gain the confidence of your banker. Don't forget, however, that you must have adequate earnings. Just getting a loan won't "save" your business.

A Tax Plan to Make Sure You Retire Rich

When I do consulting work for businesses, I continue to find owners who manage their operations with a fanatical devotion to avoiding taxes. ALL TAXES. I hate taxes, but it's a mistake to focus so much energy on minimizing taxes that writing the smallest possible check to the IRS becomes the altar upon which larger business objectives get sacrificed.

In most cases, taxes can be dramatically reduced with proper management. There are many ways to minimize taxes, most legitimate, some not so legitimate.

Instead of making all the money they can and managing their taxes, many business operators manage their income (sales) so that they have just enough to pay their expenses and live comfortably. These operators reason that if they increased sales, a large portion of the added income would go to Uncle Sam. In the meantime, they don't replace their equipment (that would trigger depreciation, a non-cash expense, and even annual write-offs, but would require an outlay of cash). Nor do they continue improving their facilities or equipment. They also don't take risks and spend money to grow the business.

Sound familiar?

Small business owners are, overall, fiscally conservative. Many of us are close to debt free, but we may be capital constrained. I would say 80 percent of the operators I've consulted for make enough to be comfortable. Yet few have a plan to make sure they stay that way when they retire.

This column is for business owners; I'm asking them to be open to the possibility of maximizing their income and investing the extra money in income-producing assets that can create a comfortable retirement.

As a consultant, I've run across some heartbreaking situations. I've seen operators who are 60 years old and unable to sell out because their operations aren't profitable with growing sales. Sadly, sometimes these owners don't sell until the business turns sour. Then, they can't or won't offer terms to a young buck who wants to try to turn it around. Often, the once-prosperous operators are left with only the value of the land their businesses occupied.

What creates these situations? Here's a common denominator: Almost all of these operators managed their businesses to avoid making TOO much money because of the tax bill the added income would trigger.

What would be so bad about doubling your annual income to $500,000, giving Uncle Sam $100,000, leaving you $400,000? That's still $150,000 more than you were going to have. If you invest the extra $150,000 in income producing assets, you'll create $3mm worth of assets over 20 years, not counting interest earned or appreciation. Even at a 10 percent return on capital, those assets would throw off $300,000 per year in perpetual income.

One operator told me he stashed away all of the money he earned beyond $300,000. For 30 years, his money was not working for him. It never appreciated, he never got any interest, and what should have been millions was still $300,000 at retirement time. That's more conservative than most of us, but aren't we doing the same thing on a lesser scale by imposing a limit on our earnings so that we won't pay too much in taxes?

It's okay to think about how to minimize your tax bill, but also think hard about how to grow your business and invest the profits in income-producing assets. Make a resolution to consider the possibility of earning a LOT MORE this year even if it means paying more in taxes.

Work with your accountant to legally shelter that income and grow it. I put most of mine in real estate. Although I seemed dumb to some people because I paid a little too much for some real estate, today, I look like a genius because the tenants have paid for the properties I purchased and now they are still producing income for me every month.

Keeping the desire to limit your tax bill in proper perspective is the first step to an even more prosperous year. How much better could you live by earning the most you can, paying the taxes you have to, and investing the surplus to create a life-long income?

Marketplace Issues
for Recyclers

Many of my columns focus specifically on issues that affect auto recyclers; this section deals with some of the toughest concerns they face today, but still offers lessons that are valuable for business owners from other areas, too.

Environmental Compliance and Competition:
Staying Focused on the Right Things

There is no doubt that it is harder to make money in the auto recycling business than it has ever been. Nevertheless, those business people who run their yards well still manage to make 10 percent or more. Some exceptionally well run yards may make as much as 20 percent. And the size of the yard isn't what makes the difference: Some have achieved these results with very large operations and some have done well on smaller volume.

These business people have succeeded by handling the details of the business that are under their direct control with great skill. They have worked hard and experimented and adapted. They have paid close attention to the marketplace and cannibalized their own business products and services to add new ones when the opportunity presented itself. These successful yards pay close attention to costs, particularly their labor costs, and they have become FULLY engaged in buying to control their cost of goods.

Business people who are unafraid to innovate and to work smart and hard run the most successful yards. They have gutted old systems and processes, they have endured lots of pain and friction, but they have tasted hard-earned success in a tough business. They are successful because they love the auto recycling business.

Other operators are not succeeding and environmental regulations are not the real reason. No doubt occasionally a shady operator undercuts them, but they are only vulnerable to that because they are not fully engaged in running their enterprises and they are not willing to make the necessary changes to stay viable. Most are doing things just as they used to and that won't get winning results in a world where the customer is a moving target.

The message of "these guys aren't competing fairly" is a dangerous one. It leads people to focus on non-core issues, and it makes yard owners and managers devote precious time and energy to things they can't impact directly, much less control.

No one would disagree that our industry association should be the main impetus for fair regulation. It's the right thing to do. However, many recyclers believe that somehow better enforcement of regulations will make them better able to be successful in the marketplace. These less successful recyclers believe that someone is going to save them or that their woes are someone else's fault. They talk constantly about their being too much competition or the competition being unfair. I've heard it for 25 years. That said, of course, we need everyone to push for fair enforcement of environmental laws.

The true costs of these controls? They aren't material in most cases. Spend some money each year on improvements and modernization, say two to three thousand dollars for a smaller yard, one selling less than $100,000 per month; then a similar amount on annual compliance and reporting. In 10 years, you will have spent $20-30,000 on controls and such. The problem develops when you spend nothing for years; it's hard when it catches up to you.

How big a problem are the environmental regulations? I believe not nearly as big as some people would like to convince you. I don't know of any recyclers that have been overly burdened by environmental controls. In fact, most yard owners embrace them and comply with them. Recyclers, like all other businesspeople, should be accountable for their own actions with regard to complying with environmental laws and their own financial results. And recyclers should support the Association in its duty to educate members on the full range of issues-some environmental and others not-that affect all of us in the recycling business today. Most of these are easy to see because we deal with them every day in our efforts to run our businesses successfully. We only need to stand in front of a mirror to see the real reason many of us aren't doing well.

I do wish we could get all recyclers to join and support the State and National Association. Full participation would make the business better for everyone.

Coping with Consolidation, Part I:
Earning Loyalty with Exceptional Customer Service

Many recyclers are wondering if larger operators will put them out of business. What will consolidation mean for you? How can you survive and compete against consolidators?

Seeing a larger competitor moving into your market isn't comforting. But before you let a Goliath throw you off your game, remember that the Davids of the world have lots of advantages. One of the advantages of being smaller is that you can respond to changes quickly.

You don't need to hold a meeting or notify partners or investors before making a change. As a sole proprietor, you are able to adapt and change far faster than the big boys can.

Nor should you forget that well-run independents can offer a level of personal service that would make many larger companies envious. The parts customer can go to a larger consolidation facility where they will be just one of the several customers in progress, or they can also come to your facility where you will take care of them personally. Being attentive to customers is an old-fashioned notion, but it's a key advantage that small recyclers can use to set themselves apart from their larger rivals.

Customers like personal attention. I know I like to get great service when I buy.

When my daughter-in-law was about 10 years old, her parents went to a store to purchase new furniture. Her father wore his gray work uniform almost everywhere. When they arrived at a large department store, her mom picked out the furniture she wanted, but none of the sales people would wait on them because they saw her father's work clothes and assumed that the family could not afford a purchase.

Her dad became frustrated and called for a salesperson. The veteran salespeople passed them off to a very green salesperson. Her dad made the purchase in cash and the reactions of those who had sought to avoid waiting on us was something that she remembers to this day.

Even at 10 years old, she noticed the lack of customer service. They were lucky that her father made a purchase at all.

When we train a new salesperson (which is not very often), we make it clear to him or her that every customer should be treated like a favorite relative or honored guest. We insist that customers get the same attention that we want when we're looking to make a purchase.

As a result, we have some very loyal customers. Some of our first customers still walk through the door or call looking for parts. It's very important when your customer comes in or calls to treat them like a guest in your home. Give them eye contact or be positive on the phone. Don't underestimate the power of being cordial, courteous and friendly to those on whose patronage your business depends. Service matters.

We have customers who call just to wish us happy holidays, customers who call that have sold their import but trust us to recommend the right place to buy an American part. With the continued growth of consolidators, small recycling facilities are likely to face even tougher competition in the future, but there will always be a place for smart recycling facilities of all sizes.

When customers call or come in for a part they like to be recognized. They like the attention. They like to know that they're dealing with service-focused people.

Whenever your phone rings, it's a customer or a potential customer with a problem. It's also an opportunity for you to shine and begin to earn a customer for life. Do the people who answer the phones at your business give the kind of service that makes customers for life?

Coping with Consolidation, Part II:
The Power of the Personal Touch

When we hear our competitor/neighbor sold to consolidators, we start wringing our hands. What are we going to do? How will we stay in business? How can we compete with the big boys that have truckloads of money?

Let's face it. The consolidators have forced our industry to do something we should have done years ago: Change, modernize, improve our systems and become sharper operators.

Worrying about consolidators and not staying focused on your business could cost you plenty. Don't fall into that trap. Stay focused on your product, improving customer service, and purchasing the correct vehicles and your customers will continue to call. Do this, not because of the consolidators, but because it makes your business better.

Consolidators have raised the bar for independents. By providing better service, quality and reliability, consolidators have made their customers comfortable with salvaged parts. They have forced smaller facilities to improve the perception of salvaged parts by washing parts before delivering or adding some type of accreditation program (URG8000, Goldseal, etc.).

Consolidators have purchased recycling facilities coast to coast to give themselves the opportunity to sell more parts and buy more parts vehicles. However, we have the same opportunity with URG, Car-Part, and Eden. We trade with independent recyclers without the overhead of distribution trucks, employees, and expenses. Here are two possible paths forward: Join with your local competitors to lower your expenses by sharing fees for buyers, deliveries and employees; or consider joining an independent consolidation group in your region. Independent recyclers become stronger by working together.

Nor should you let the fear of consolidators rule your decision-making. We have certain advantages in being small businesses. We are closer to the customer and have more direct control over our enterprises than larger businesses do. A well-managed small business can be far more nimble in the marketplace because it has fewer layers of management.

Also, do you really think that size allows consolidators an edge when buying inventory, which is the single biggest component of our cost? I don't.

Imagine listening in on salvage yard owners discussing the state of business 10 years ago. What were they saying then? The same thing that they are saying now. Business is tough. They were making the same complaint you hear now, but for different reasons.

I was around a decade ago when state legislatures were passing salvage title laws. The cars at the pools, as well as pool fees, were skyrocketing and all recyclers were concerned. People said we wouldn't survive, but we are more profitable today than we were then, at least at my facility. Sometimes it is hard to see the solutions. We just want things to be the way they used to be.

The solutions are out there. Network with other salvage yard owners, and ask how they are lowering costs. It can be done. I know, because we have continued to lower our cost year after year, using the same techniques we teach our consulting clients every day.

Tips & Tools

Small business owners are always looking for ways to save time and money. These columns look at a few ways I have found to do both. I'll end this section with a list of some of the best time-saving tools I've discovered.

Power in the Palm of Your Hand: PDAs for Small Business Owners

Small business people are the busiest people on the planet. Growing a small business requires entrepreneurs to find ways to do more in less time.

My PDA helps me get more done. Few pieces of technology have saved me more hours than my Treo PDA. In fact, I feel so strongly about the value of PDAs that I have all of my managers carry them.

When we need to contact an employee, all managers have a master list of the latest staff contact information in their PDAs. It's a huge time saver.

Personally, I have found my PDA to be a great help in doing more with less time.

•   **Scheduling Appointments:** I am easily able to make an appointment without hunting for a paper organizer to see if I have a conflict. The reminder makes certain that I never miss a scheduled appointment.

•   **Saving Time in Tax Planning:** Keeping everything in the PDA makes providing needed information to tax professionals much simpler.

•   **Updating and Keeping Contacts Organized:** When I run into an old friend, I am always able to easily capture new contact information and keep it at my fingertips. So much of what I have accomplished in business has been because of my ability to call on the right people quickly. For example, when I needed to re-capitalize my business in the late 1990s with a private stock offering, I had over 1,000 names of friends, family, bankers, and business acquaintances in my PDA. The power of my PDA to capture and keep contacts current was key to oversubscribing the offering in two weeks.

•   **Note Taking During Management by Walking Around** - My PDA has helped me make clear notes when I am out of my office managing by walking around. The virtual pad feature of my PDA has helped me capture ideas in areas where writing them down isn't practical.

•   **Creating Meeting Agendas on the Fly** - For entrepreneurs holding weekly management meetings, a PDA is an excellent tool for gathering and organizing items on the fly. I created meeting agendas on my PDA, and each week, as new things came up that needed to be addressed in the meeting, I entered them. Just before the meeting, I'd cut and paste the list into a Word document and print it out! After the meeting, I'd edit and remove items addressed, and create the new agenda for the following week right on the PDA. Staff members were attentive to assigned *to dos* because of how well our agenda-driven weekly meeting worked. The PDA certainly helped me delegate and follow up more effectively on tasks assigned.

Effective small business management requires state-of-the-art time management tools. If you're still using a paper calendar and address book, it's time to try a PDA.

Three Secrets to Awakening Your Passion for Business

Passion - where did it go? Many folks I talk to say, "It's just not fun anymore." That can be the case. But where did that competitive spirit go? I think business is just as much fun, but the bar has certainly been raised.

By now, most of you know that I am one of the team members that bought GreenLeaf and am a key part of the management team. Why did I do it? My wife says I am a glutton for punishment.

But I have a different reason: Passion.

Several of my articles this year have discussed passion. Those who know me understand my passion for business and how I make it part of all my endeavors. I am unrelenting in my desire to reach a goal. That driving passion is part of my management style that encompasses the following three principles:

Manage by objective but hold nothing back - I often see folks wringing their hands because they didn't hit a goal and expressing remorse over some things that they *could or should have done*. Not me. When I decide to do something, I decide what it takes. I hold nothing back. You can accuse me of being over the top, but never of holding back. If I don't hit the goal, I *never* have remorse that I did less than I could have. I *know* I did everything humanly possible to make it happen; so I have no regrets. This all-out approach allows me to turn the corner and go on when I fail.

Choose battles carefully - I don't try to change something I can't change or attempt something I know I can't do. Life is too short, and energies are too precious to waste on fruitless endeavors. It's that simple.

Be a skilled listener and consensus builder - I didn't learn this until I had been in business about 10 years. I thought I knew all the answers. I didn't. I learned to listen better. Some folks were kinder, more diplomatic, and knew the financials better or simply had a different (and sometimes better) perspective. I met industry experts like Don Egilseer (Smart Parts), Al & Ed Lacy, Herb Lieberman, Garry Howard, Stu Willen, Howard Nussbaum, Ken Vonhoff, Don Fitz, Jr., even Barry Isenberg, and the list goes on and on. When several of us get together and work on an idea, and agree, it's almost always a better product than any of us could have produced working alone.

Freeze!: Protect Yourself from Identity Theft

Imagine receiving a visit from a local sheriff with a handful of your mail that he retrieved from a ditch. Consider how it would feel to get a welcome call from an account representative at a store in a city 1,000 miles away verifying that you have opened a charge account.

The Federal Trade Commission estimates that 9 million Americans have their identities stolen every year. If you are a high profile person in your community, your odds just increased.

Identity thieves target me about three times a year, so I have learned a few simple steps to protect myself. It may be prudent for you to put a fraud alert or a freeze on your credit bureaus.

With a police report, you can place a permanent fraud alert on your reports. Before new credit is issued, the issuing company will call you at the number you provide to the bureaus and verify the legitimacy of the request. Without a police report, a temporary fraud alert can be placed on your file for 90 days. With a police report, the alert lasts up to seven years.

To place a fraud alert, call one of the three credit bureaus, or go to their web sites:

*   Equifax: 800-525-6285, www.equifax.com
*   Experian: 888-397-3742, www.experian.com
*   TransUnion: 800-680-7289, www.teansunion.com

By asking the credit bureaus to do this, you ensure that only businesses that you have an established relationship with can see your credit file. Before issuing any new credit, the credit issuer must speak to you personally at the number that you provided to the bureaus. It's far better to learn about an attempted identity theft before any damage has been done.

However, I recently had a reminder of how this added protection can have a downside. I purchased a new Apple iPhone. It took me days to get it activated because we had reshuffled the extensions in my office and I didn't update the credit bureaus in writing of my new contact number.

The credit issuer will ONLY speak to you at the number you have provided the bureaus. The onus is on you to remember to update the bureaus when you make a change. Despite this drawback, it is worth considering putting a fraud alert on your credit file.

The other option is to freeze your report. A freeze allows you to restrict access to your report. It is a good solution for people who want to protect themselves from identity theft and who do not regularly apply for credit.

The downside: A freeze takes a few days to lift, so freezing your credit can cost you if you need to apply for credit quickly. A freeze means only companies with which you have a business relationship can see your report. To get new credit, you must notify the bureaus and lift the freeze. You can lift it across the board if you are shopping around or lift it only for a specific creditor to look at your report.

To put a freeze on your report, send certified letters with proof of identity and address and $10, or a copy of the police report, to:

• Equifax Security Freeze. P.O. Box 105788, Atlanta, GA 30348

• TransUnion Fraud Victim Assistance Dept., P.O. Box 6790, Fullerton, CA 92834

• Experian Security Freeze P.O. Box 9554, Allen, TX 75013

A credit report freeze on all three of your reports will cost $30.83 in Texas. It varies by state because sales tax is added to the $10, but the bureaus will freeze your report for free if you have a police report. The cost to temporarily thaw your credit report ranges from zero to $12, depending on the bureau. A report can be temporarily "thawed" if you need an employer, lender, insurer or anyone else to have access to your report. Again, no police report is required.

When Minutes Are Precious, Try These Time-Saving Tools

• **Google News Alerts** - Did you know you can use Google to watch for articles of interest, using keywords? Google will search for your keywords and email you the results daily. Try using your name, or LKQ, or auto recycling. Setting up alerts is simple.

• **PDA Power** - I am an avid user of a PDA (personal digital assistant). I started with a Palm and now am using a Treo. Having my cell phone and PDA in a single unit allows me to carry one device and never worry about synchronizing address books. If you've never tried using a PDA, you'll be amazed at how much more productive one can make you.

• **Roboform** - Tired of logging onto all those websites

(including Copart and eBay)? Are you finding your passwords are getting more numerous and difficult to manage? Are you annoyed by entering the same information in online order forms? I use a program called Roboform. A basic version, which is likely all you need, is available at www.roboform.com. This utility will automatically fill out all those forms for you and remember all your passwords. You can visit a new website to order something and complete the order in just a few seconds! It saves your personal and business identities and protects them with a single master password.

• **Google's Desktop Search Tool** - Tired of waiting and waiting for the Microsoft search function to find your files? Want to be able to search your emails for a key phrase? Microsoft's utility won't, but the Google desktop search tool will. Find it this great free tool at http://desktop.google.com. It allows you to use the same tricks that you use with Google to find files stored on your computer.

• **Public Records Search Tool** - Check out the public records on your company or yourself at www.searchsystems.net.

• **Four-in-One Memory Card Reader** - I have several different electronic devices that use memory cards, so I use a four-in-one card reader. No need for cables for all your devices and it's just easier to use. Simply put the card from any of your devices into the reader and it's ready to read or write to. These newer readers are very inexpensive; I paid $15 at Circuit City. Don't buy a card reader that only reads one type of card when the four-in-one reader is available for the same price.

• **Trick for Keeping Track of Registrations and Purchases** - I created an email folder for "computer stuff and orders." You know...you ordered something but then can't find where or when, to resolve a dispute or non-receipt. When I am on the web site at the order page, I simply send myself the page and put in the subject line the pertinent words. If the page can't be sent, I darken it for a copy and paste it into the body of an email I send myself. Tired of looking for those product registration numbers? Send them to yourself in an email. If you ever have to reload a program, you will know right where to find your registration key.

Index

G

Georg, Clint 37
goal(s) 26, 33-37, 47, 50-51, 57, 88, 108, 153, 227
goal setting 35, 51
Goliath 261
good banker 59, 65
Google News Alerts 271
gross sales 35, 216

H

habit(s) 113, 137, 140, 147, 152-154, 158, 166, 213
hidden benefits 55
hidden wealth 202
high-service provider 45
high value provider 242
how to generate sales 87
Howard, Garry 269
Hughes, Howard 209
human nature 235

I

identity theft 269
image 113-114, 191
inability 247
Inc. Magazine 228
incentive 121
incentives 128
increase sales 88, 91, 98
independents 263
industry association 262
industry standards 5
initiative(s) 227, 238
innovate 261
integrity 148
intellectual property 229
interest rates 258
internal benchmarks 25
internal guarantees 132
internet and web presence 228
interview 221, 223

M

N

N(*continued*)

niche holders 116
non-core issues 262
non-performing employees 46
Nordstom 242
numbers 84-85, 94, 101
Nussbaum, Howard 269

O

obstacles 96
one footitis 244
operating metrics 1, 4-7, 10, 13, 29, 46, 101, 215, 225, 227, 243
operational plans 252
outgoing marketing 37
overcome obstacles 96
ownership 202-203

P

Palm Pilot 167
passion 145-154, 159, 167, 268
pay for performance 232, 227, 248
PDA 52-54, 162, 267
peer relationships 134-135
peers 241
perception 115, 117, 133
performance 120-121, 125
perseverance 150, 211
persevering attitude 153, 157-160, 213
Personal Digital Assistant 52-54, 162
philosophical 253
phone system 245
Pinnacle system 242
plan 29, 31-34, 57-59, 137, 146, 210
planning 27-31, 34-36, 53, 56, 78
pocket notepad (see PDA) 52
point of contact 129
point of poor return 83
point of sale 96
position yourself 143-144
positive image 116

S

V

value 254vendors 127
vision 140, 147, 210, 213
Vonhoff, Ken 269
VW Bug 144

W

Wal-Mart 242
warranties 106, 193-194, 242
watermelon story 239
weak employees 244
weaknesses 208, 211
weighing the upside gain against the downside risk 200
who, what, when, why and where 36
wholesale 241
Willen, Stu 269
Williams, Walter 160
work ethic 126, 139, 157, 213, 247
work performance 107
workable solution 227
written plan 236, 237

Y

Yellow Pages 228
you don't know what you don't know 251
Yudkin, Marcia 74-75

Author

About the author Ron Sturgeon

Although he didn't start with many secret advantages, Ron Sturgeon has always had a nose for opportunity and a knack for entrepreneurship. When his father died, his stepmother threw 17-year-old Ron out of the house. Homeless but undeterred, Ron parlayed a $1500 inheritance and a used VW into a successful auto repair business right out of high school.

The repair business grew into one of the largest auto salvage businesses in the United States. Never afraid to innovate, Ron developed new marketing techniques and was the first to computerize his operation. Inc Magazine profiled his business because of Ron's ability use database driven direct marketing intelligently to grow his company. Using simple tools, Ron created a system that worked to find and close high value accounts efficiently.

When Ron needed capital to expand, he did his first oversubscribed private stock offering. In 1999, Ford brought Ron's six yard, 140-employee Texas operation.

In 2001, Ron founded an auto auction to help insurance companies in Texas dispose of salvaged vehicles. Again, Ron sought investors in a private stock offering and again it was oversubscribed. Fifteen months later, the largest public company in the sector purchased his company. Drawing on his experiences, Ron wrote How to Salvage Millions from Your Small Business, a guide for entrepreneurs, now in its third printing and licensed in five other languages.

In 2003, Ron and two partners purchased Ford Motor Company's auto salvage division. GreenLeaf had grown to 26 locations in 15 states and over 1,000 employees, but it was losing over a million dollars per month. Ron was in charge of legal, environmental, insurance, licenses and permits after the buyback. He held a board seat and contributed to improving sales and marketing, lowering costs in purchasing, and implementing better employee training programs.

After turning around the operation, Ron and his partners sold to a $2 billion dollar public company in 2005.. Ron's second book, Green Weenies and Due Diligence an insider's guide to the colorful lexicon of the boardroom, was published in 2005.

Ron's current ventures include an exotic car rental company in Fort Worth, managing his commercial real estate holdings and a full schedule of business consulting and public speaking on topics related to successful entrepreneurship.